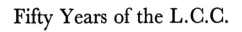

Fifty Years of the L.C.C.

Fifty Years of the L.C.C.

by

S. P. B. MAIS

Drawings by
KUPFER-SACHS

Cambridge
at the University Press
1939

CAMBRIDGE
UNIVERSITY PRESS

University Printing House, Cambridge CB2 8BS, United Kingdom

Cambridge University Press is part of the University of Cambridge.

It furthers the University's mission by disseminating knowledge in the pursuit of education, learning and research at the highest international levels of excellence.

www.cambridge.org
Information on this title: www.cambridge.org/9781107452589

© Cambridge University Press 1939

First published 1939
First paperback edition 2014

A catalogue record for this publication is available from the British Library

ISBN 978-1-107-45258-9 Paperback

Contents

Chapter 1. The L.C.C.   *page* 9

2. Other London Services   26

3. London's Money   32

4. London's Schools   36

5. London's Houses   52

6. London's Greens   69

7. London's Buildings   85

8. London's Roads   90

9. London's Poor   94

10. London's Health   105

11. London's Blind   131

12. London's Fire Brigade   134

13. London's Protection   146

14. London's Supplies   156

List of Books   160

Illustrations

County Hall: the seat of London's Government
to-day (*Fox photo*)   *facing p.* 10

The Battersea Power Station (*copyright The London
Power Company*)   11

Old County Hall: the seat of London's Government yesterday (*copyright L.C.C.*)   14

The first meeting of the L.C.C., from *The Graphic*,
Feb. 1889 (*copyright The Sphere*)   15

A horse-bus: one of the first motor-buses
(*copyright L.P.T.B.*)   18

The noisy horse-tram (*Topical Press photo*): a modern
70-seater trolley-bus (*copyright L.P.T.B.*)   19

East India Docks 1892: Dock scene 1893
(*Rischgitz photos*)   22

The Pool—Royal Albert Docks: London Bridge
(*Fox photos*)   23

London schoolboys, Bermondsey 1894: Bermondsey schoolboys in 1934 (*copyrights L.C.C.*)   38

School playgrounds—Junior and Senior Elementary (*copyrights L.C.C.*)   39

Mothercraft: School Library (*copyrights L.C.C.*)   42

The workshop of a Technical Institute: the
garden of a Girls' Secondary School (*copyrights L.C.C.*)   43

Sidney Street slum (*copyright The St Pancras House
Improvement Society*)   54

Rebuilding London—Lambeth Bridge old and
new (*photos L.C.C. and Fox*)   55

Whitmore Estate: before clearance, and to-day—
Rover House (*copyrights L.C.C.*)   58

Modern block dwellings—Clapham Park Estate
    and Oaklands Estate (*copyrights L.C.C.*)   *facing p.* 59
Houses on the street, old and new plan—Essex
    Street, Hoxton, and Roehampton estate
    (*Times and L.C.C. photos*)   68
An Epping Forest glade (*Fox photo*)   69
Kennington Park Swimming Pool (*Photopress*):
    Victoria Embankment Playing Ground (*Fox
    photo*)   72
Cricket—in a Hoxton alley (*Topical Press photo*)
    and on Parliament Hill Fields (*Fox photo*)   73
Regent Street 1898: Oxford Street to-day
    (*photos Rischgitz, L.P.T.B.*)   88
They seemed to get more sun at Charing Cross in
    1890 (*photo Rischgitz*)   89
Waterloo Bridge—as it will be (*copyright L.C.C.*):
    and as it was (*photo Rischgitz*)   92
Thames tunnel: Woolwich Ferry (*copyrights L.C.C.*)   93
Public Assistance Institution nursery
    (*copyright L.C.C.*)   132
High Wood Hospital (*copyright L.C.C.*)   133
The old Tooting Fire Station and Fire Brigade
    Headquarters to-day (*copyrights L.C.C.*)   140
A fire on the wharf (*Planet News photo*)   141
Fire in the City (*Central Press photo*)   150
Galloping to the rescue—the old Fire Brigade
    (*Topical Press photo*): a modern Fire Engine
    (*copyright L.C.C.*)   151
Weights and Measures Inspectors (*photos Keystone
    Press, Black Star*)   154
"Whitehall 1212" (*copyright The Metropolitan
    Police*): how London protects its citizens
    (*Graphic Photo Union*)   155

Maps

London's Green Belt   *front endpaper*

The Growth of London   *back endpaper*

London's Main Roads   *between pp. 80 and 81*

London's Areas   *between pp. 112 and 113*

Chapter 1   THE L.C.C.

Have you ever crossed Westminster Bridge?

If you have crossed it in a tram or bus you probably got little chance to see any of the many things that are worth stopping to see from there. If you have crossed it on foot you have probably gone at the speed of the rest of the walkers in order not to get jostled by people overtaking you.

What you should do is to get up early one September morning, and just stand on the bridge and watch the sun rise over the river and the houses before the hum of traffic and the crowds get in the way of your seeing what there is to see and hearing what there is to hear.

William Wordsworth, the poet, saw London in this way early one September morning about 140 years ago, and he was so startled by the beauty of what he saw that he composed this sonnet about it:

> *Earth has not anything to show more fair:*
> *Dull would he be of soul who could pass by*
> *A sight so touching in its majesty:*
> *This city now doth like a garment wear*
> *The beauty of the morning; silent, bare,*
> *Ships, towers, domes, theatres, and temples lie*
> *Open unto the fields, and to the sky;*
> *All bright and glittering in the smokeless air.*
> *Never did sun more beautifully steep*
> *In his first splendour valley, rock, or hill;*
> *Ne'er saw I, never felt, a calm so deep!*
> *The river glideth at his own sweet will:*
> *Dear God! The very houses seem asleep;*
> *And all that mighty heart is lying still!*

This very high praise is all the more remarkable coming as it did from a poet who found his inspiration almost entirely in the remote hills and rivers of the Lake District.

He was not in the least like his friend Charles Lamb, who was never happy away from the street lamps and bustle of the busy London streets.

And yet this country lover could say of London

> *Earth has not anything to show more fair.*

It was, of course, a very different London from the London that you and I see from Westminster Bridge.

In the first place he talks about the smokeless air, and in spite of the coming of electricity one of London's main problems to-day is to reduce the amount of smoke in the air.

The buildings which were not there in Wordsworth's time, the Houses of Parliament, for instance, still stand

County Hall: the seat of London's Government to-day

One of London's loveliest sights—the Battersea Power Station

open to the sky, but it is no longer easy to see any fields from Westminster Bridge.

But one curious thing you will notice if you stand on the bridge on any early morning when the sun is just beginning to lighten up the walls and roof-tops. It does seem in its quietness unexpectedly countrified.

There is width and space and plenty of room to breathe. That of course is partly due to the great breadth of the Thames just here. A river always has a country atmosphere about it and the new buildings along the north and south banks add to its majesty. Between Shell-Mex House and Battersea Power Station, two excellent examples of the simple grandeur of modern architecture, you will see not only in the Southern Railway Depot, W. H. Smith and Sons, and the L.C.C. Fire Brigade Headquarters, but also and most of all in the crescent-shaped County Hall, the seat of London's government, buildings which add very considerably to the beauty of the scene.

If what you saw from here were the whole of London nobody could deny its claim to be the fairest city in the world.

But a contemporary of William Wordsworth, one William Cobbett, saw another London, which so disgusted him by its ugliness that he christened it the Great Wen, or Wart.

And it is a great Wen in so far as it has grown without being properly shaped. It sprawled over the country places that had once been sporting Marylebone and isolated Islington, where men went to shoot game, and cattle grazed in peace.

Some cities are planned before being built. All the streets and avenues of Washington, for example, irradiate from the Capitol (the American House of Parliament), like the spokes of a bicycle wheel from its axis.

But London "just growed", like Topsy.

The result is that it is very difficult for strangers to find their way about.

One very observant foreigner has described London as "a shapeless mass dumped down as circumstances dictated according to the lie of the country, the biggest port and biggest business centre in existence, a gigantic pleasure resort, the city of the richest and of the poorest of the poor, the homes of all nations, full of unspeakable monotony and unbelievable variety".

You may very well wonder why this great unwieldy mass which sprawls over six counties should have grown just here, and equally wonder why it has become the greatest city in the world.

Before the Romans came London was a marshy tract merging into a primeval forest, but under their rule it rose within a very short time to be a flourishing trading centre which, after its destruction by Boadicea, was soon rebuilt and fortified by a strong wall, the remains of which you can still see.

When the Romans left in A.D. 410 London slipped back into decay. Its streets were deserted for over a hundred years, but by the beginning of the seventh century the ancient bishopric was revived as the result of the visit of St Augustine.

The Abbey of Westminster was founded in the eighth century in the Isle of Thorney, a long way out of London, and rebuilt by King Edward the Confessor, who also built himself a palace close by.

William the Conqueror had himself crowned in this Abbey and lived in this Palace.

He then built the White Tower, the heart of the present Tower, to remind the citizens of London of his presence and power, but he had the wisdom also to please them by giving them a charter of liberties.

So during the Middle Ages London became rich and important and overflowed beyond the Roman and Norman walls and gates to new gates and bars in Temple Bar and Holborn Bar.

Westminster also grew more important after Henry II fixed the Law Courts there.

Noblemen built houses along the south side of the Strand and in Westminster, and very soon the richer merchants followed their example.

Both Elizabeth and James I tried to stop further encroachments on London's countryside without much avail, though St Martin's and St Giles both remained in the fields for a long time.

Then, as the result of the Plague and Fire, London had to be rebuilt, and a displaced population found accommodation outside, and the richer merchants began to build country houses in the tiny villages of St Pancras, Stepney, Islington, and so on.

Then the building in the late eighteenth century of Westminster and Blackfriars Bridges led to the development of the south side of the river.

More than one-fifth of all the people in England and Wales live in London.

The reason for its popularity is that, owing to the convenience of its position as a port, it has become the market town of the world. The feature you notice least, its docks, is the feature that gives London its industrial pre-eminence.

The river remained London's highway for many centuries, and in Shakespeare's time all the theatres were huddled together along the south bank at Southwark.

In Stuart times there were half a million inhabitants and it had reached a stage where growth was checked by the difficulty of supplying fresh food and horse-fodder from the surrounding country and by the difficulty of getting good drinking-water. The water from the streams of Tyburn and Fleet was so bad that it only served to spread the plague.

In 1613 the "New River" was constructed to bring the clear chalk water from Hertfordshire. It wasn't until much later that they learnt to bore through the London clay to the chalk beneath that now produces London's excellent drinking-water.

The rich built mansions along all the river banks, as the river was the only link with London, the roads being impassable in winter owing to the sodden London clay.

Then came the turnpikes and the improvements of Telford and McAdam which made transport easy, and soon merchants began to drive daily from their suburban homes to their work in the city.

Buildings spread from the gravel terraces to the damp London clay north of the Marylebone and Euston roads. There was an attempt to plan out certain western suburbs in Belgravia and Bloomsbury in squares and wide streets.

The royal parks, Hyde Park, Green Park and St James's Park, formed the western limit of building until George IV's reign. Beyond them the West Bourne flowed across the wet fields. Then the architect Cubitt discovered that the clay was only a thin sheet covering an older bed of gravel, so he cleverly peeled off the silt, and turned it into bricks for houses, which he built on the gravel that lay below. This accounts for Regent Street, Portland Place, Trafalgar Square and adjacent streets.

The east end was, however, left to sprawl as it liked all over the low-lying marshes round the newly constructed docks, and on the south side only the Embankments saved the crowded areas of Lambeth Marsh from being flooded.

Then came the railways, enlarging the rim of the circumference of accessibility very considerably, reducing

Old County Hall: the seat of London's Government yesterday

The men who first governed London. A cartoon of the first meeting of the L.C.C., February 1889

the population of the city and immensely increasing the population of all areas up to a radius of at least thirty miles out. There were people of course who were too poor to get out, and this has meant that in an area like Shoreditch 100,000 people are packed into a square mile.

One tide of people swarmed northward up the clay slopes towards the heights of Highgate and Hampstead. They reached Hornsey, Crouch End and Muswell Hill about 1880.

Then in 1907, ashamed of the shapeless sprawling, they planned garden suburbs in Golder's Green.

The wide marshy valley on the east of the river Lea prevented expansion that way at first, so the drive was northwards to Tottenham and Edmonton. But in 1850 West Ham began to spread over Plaistow Marsh, and Stratford became a suburb.

Later development spread fan-wise from Stratford Broadway north to Walthamstow, and east across the river Roding to Ilford.

In the West End slums began to spring up near Sloane Street, but as the West End spread to Knightsbridge and South Kensington the slums were replaced by richer houses. Campden Hill was already dotted about with country mansions in the seventeenth and eighteenth centuries.

When the spread reached Hammersmith it joined up again with the old riverside villages that had always been the resort of the rich.

The southern suburbs developed by two leaps, first to the gravel tops of the southern plateau and then to the foot of the North Downs.

This has meant that London has spread a very considerable way out southward, but there are gaps of open spaces westward from Blackheath, at Peckham Rye,

Brockwell Park, Clapham, Tooting and Wandsworth Common to break the line of continuous building, and beyond the Wandle Valley still stand Putney Heath, Wimbledon Common and Richmond Park, which form the largest area of open country in London County.

On the south side about two miles of low-lying land have to be crossed between Lambeth and the Surrey Docks before you reach the plateau, and before the railways came this was all built up. Then came the railways, and it was left vacant until about 1880, when building re-started.

Whenever you leave London by train on the north side you immediately plunge into tunnels, whereas on the south side you travel along the tops of causeways and embankments overlooking the slate roofs of innumerable houses. That shows you how the land tilts down from north to south.

Then comes the plateau of Dulwich village, which is still a village in spite of being only four miles from London, and east and west of it stand Forest Hill, Tulse Hill, Brixton Hill and Clapham, which were all covered with suburban houses when the railway was built.

Farther south at the foot of the North Downs stands Croydon, in 1801 a little market town of 5000 inhabitants, now risen to 200,000 by reason of the railway.

The making of new arterial roads brought into being a new type of ribbon development, and new suburbs sprang up along both sides of all the new roads, thereby completely defeating the object of the roads.

All this formless sprawling has meant an extraordinarily complicated form of government.

There are no fewer than 355 authorities concerned with the control of London, so that there is bound to be a certain amount of confusion.

North Harrow, for instance, has a parish council at Pinner, a rural council at Harrow Weald, a county council (Middlesex) at Westminster, a police court at Wealdstone, a bankruptcy court at St Albans, a county court at Watford, a head post-office at Harrow, a gas supply from south-west London, electricity supply from north London, a water-supply from Bushey, a workhouse at Edgware, a parish church at Pinner, a bishop at Willesden and a member of Parliament at Hendon.

That gives you some idea of the difficulties confronting the London County Council in looking after this vast area.

In the old days London was just the City of London, an area of one square mile which has never expanded.

In Saxon days London was ruled by a portreeve and bishop. In Henry I's reign the citizens were allowed to elect their own shire-reeve (sheriff). In King John's reign came the first government by mayor, twelve aldermen and twelve "other men of probity".

The names of these rulers still remain in the streets of Bucklersbury, Farringdon, Pountney Hill and Basinghall Street.

Owing to murders and riots Edward I appointed a "custos" or warden to restore order, but the mayoralty was restored in 1297 and has continued ever since. When the mayor began to be called Lord Mayor is not known. His jurisdiction never extended beyond the City of London.

The London that we know is made up mainly of the villages and towns that lay outside the City, and these were controlled by their own vestries, working through unpaid officials, the parish constable, the surveyor of highways, and the overseers of the poor, with various district boards and commissioners of sewers and paving and so on.

As the City dwindled Outer London grew. In 1801 the

population of the London we know was 830,000 and that of the City 128,000.

By 1889 London's population had risen to 4,000,000 and the City had dwindled to 40,000.

Something had to be done to bring this vast mass under one control.

When Sir Benjamin Hall was fighting for this reform he pointed out that in the Strand alone there were eleven miles of streets with no less than seven different bodies responsible for its paving, each with its own establishment of clerks, collectors, surveyors and other officers. One of the surveyors was a tailor and another a law stationer. It was costing ratepayers £88 a mile just to maintain the staffs. In St Pancras, out of 472 commissioners 255 were self-elected and they had set up fourteen public pumps, one of which was out of order, for a population of 170,000.

So the first step taken towards unifying the services was the foundation in 1855 of the Metropolitan Board of Works, which was mainly concerned with drainage.

Its members were elected by the City Corporation, the vestries of the twenty-three larger parishes, and the fourteen district boards under which the smaller parishes had been grouped.

It is due to the work of this Board that London's drainage is so well systematised.

But charges of corruption were brought against them, and after a Royal Commission had made an enquiry the Metropolitan Board of Works became merged into the new London County Council, whose jubilee has now been reached.

The City of London was left as it was to be ruled by its own Corporation.

But the London County Council took over the manage-

Above: A horse-bus

Below: One of the first motor-buses

Above: The noisy horse-tram

Below: Comfort and efficiency of travel—a modern 70-seater trolley-bus

ment of the whole of the rest of the Metropolitan Board of Works area, and is now responsible for the welfare of nearly 4½ million people.

So its foundation in 1889, two of the most important of its duties, education and the relief of the poor, were still left in the hands of other bodies, the London School Board, created in 1869, the ancient Boards of Guardians, and the modern Metropolitan Asylums Board.

Education was taken over by the L.C.C. in 1904 and Poor Relief in 1930.

In 1899 the London Boroughs, based on the old parishes, were created to look after such work as can be better administered locally.

This means that London County really consists of twenty-nine towns who entrust their main welfare to the L.C.C. but look after their internal affairs themselves.

You may be wondering what the L.C.C. does.

It is responsible for the health, education and well-being of 4½ million people, which is a bigger population than Denmark or Switzerland.

It spends £40,000,000 a year, which sounds a good deal until you remember that it looks after 117 square miles of the most closely packed community imaginable and that over £30,000,000 goes in keeping up rate services, mental hospitals and housing.

Its income is £21,740,771 through rates, nearly £9,000,000 in grants from the Government, and £3,500,000 from rents for its houses.

It controls over a thousand schools, in which there are nearly half a million boys and girls, in addition to a further quarter of a million who are being trained in the technical evening schools.

It owns 86,756 dwellings which house a population of 380,958.

It controls sixty-two fire brigade stations which quell 10,000 fires a year, disposes annually of 106,014 million gallons of sewage, looks after 30,000 mentally defective patients, and a further 30,000 patients in general and other hospitals, at a cost of £5,500,000 a year, provides 104 parks covering 6658 acres, runs sixteen accident section stations and six general ambulance section stations with 173 ambulances, gives public assistance to 72,900 poor persons in their own homes and 10,000 more in institutions at a cost of £7,000,000 a year, and tests about two million weights and measures. It keeps up the river walls of the embankments, ten bridges over the Thames and four tunnels under it, supervises the safety of the public at over 800 theatres and cinemas, issues motor licences, tests gas and supplies milk at ½d. a day to half a million children.

There are 144 members of the Council, 124 being councillors elected every three years, the remaining twenty being aldermen who hold office for six years.

They meet nearly every Tuesday in a very handsome horseshoe-shaped meeting-hall known as the County Hall, which is situated on the south side of Westminster Bridge. It was begun in 1909 and opened by H.M. King George V in 1922. It cost £3,636,533.

There are nine floors with about a thousand rooms, the most notable being the council chamber, libraries, conference hall and members' and committee rooms.

There is a staff of 76,500, 18,000 of whom are teachers, 2000 members of the fire brigade, 22,000 in the hospitals, 3000 in the housing estates, 8000 in the mental hospitals service, 1450 in the parks service, 3100 in the public assistance service, and 1000 in the main drainage service.

Most of the 6000 on the control staff are at County Hall, but the Fire Brigade Headquarters is on the Albert Embankment, the Parks Department is at Golden Cross

House, Strand, the Supplies in Shell-Mex and the Valuer is to be found in the Old County Hall, Spring Gardens.

Most of the L.C.C. members serve on one or more of the seventeen committees, of which the most important are the Housing and Public Health, Education, Hospitals and Medical Services, Public Assistance and Finance, the Parks, Highways and Entertainments.

As you see from the list of its main activities the L.C.C. makes it its business to protect the interest of all London's citizens from the cradle to the grave.

It takes the part of nurse, teacher, foster-parent, guardian and philanthropist in turn.

It tries to reduce accident and sickness and to help those who fall victim to either.

It ensures that when old age overtakes a Londoner he or she can be certain of being looked after.

What is distressing is the fact that so many Londoners should live in such a state of poverty that they are unable to save up enough to live on in old age, and that even in this very healthy town there should be such a great deal of physical and mental disease.

What it amounts to is that we are paying for the sins and errors of our fathers, and that the L.C.C. has shouldered a burden which would not have been there had the earlier Government of London been in the hands of a body possessed of a fiftieth part of its sense of re-sponsibility or its efficiency.

What is to me most extraordinary is that a body dealing as it does with millions of pounds and millions of people, confronted with so many problems of great magnitude, should yet find time to concentrate on so many points of minute detail as the L.C.C. does.

The L.C.C. in spite of its size is the most human official body that I have encountered.

It is very accessible.

Did you know that you can yourself attend the meetings on Tuesday afternoons in County Hall if you wish?

Did you know that you can obtain free admission to the Wednesday afternoon displays by the Fire Brigade at the headquarters on the Albert Embankment, where there is room for 800 spectators?

Did you know that you can get one of the best-cooked meals in London at the Hotel and Restaurant Technical School at the Westminster Technical Institute?

Did you know that in Victoria Park in east London the L.C.C. runs the finest "Lido" in the country?

Did you know that at Avery Hill, Eltham, the L.C.C. has provided the largest Palm Houses and Greenhouses outside Kew?

Have you ever seen the ornamental plaques on London houses telling you the names and dates of famous men and women who have lived in them? The L.C.C. has been responsible for them.

Do you know that in a hundred L.C.C. schools the children exchange letters with the officers and men of ships that they have adopted as friends?

Do you realise that the L.C.C. is carrying out a complete reform of street names in order to solve the difficulty of duplicates in street names?

Do you know that fifty school playgrounds are kept open on summer evenings with special games-leaders? And that they are floodlit for games on winter evenings?

Do you know that the L.C.C. runs a Supplies Department to buy cheaply in bulk exactly what it wants for all its many activities: over a million pounds of bacon, over eight million of eggs, 28 million pints of milk and so on?

By this means it is possible to maintain a patient in a hospital for 4s. a week.

Above: East India Docks 1892
Below: Dock scene 1893

Above: The Pool—Royal Albert Docks
Below: London Bridge—from here they sail to the Seven Seas

Do you know that young or old who find themselves friendless in London can join the City Literary Institute, where they can choose from no fewer than 269 courses of lectures and join innumerable social clubs?

Do you know that no one, however poor, need ever sleep out in London, that a bed is ready for any destitute man who applies at the L.C.C. Welfare Office?

The L.C.C. is not at all the sort of body to rest on its laurels.

During the crisis of September–October 1938 the Education Department gave a memorable lead to the country in carrying out with complete success an evacuation scheme which meant the moving of an army of well over half a million children divided among nearly 3000 school departments and spread over an area of about 200 square miles. Every parent had been consulted, every railway time-table fixed, every school ready to move to an appointed station at an appointed hour to be conveyed to an area where full preparations had been made for their coming.

Twenty thousand teachers were in charge and ready to move off on the receipt of a code telegram.

Actually 2100 physically defective children were evacuared on Wednesday, 28 September, and 1200 nursery school children and 1000 blind and deaf children on Thursday, 29 September. They were all back in London again within a week.

In addition to this, 2000 patients in eighteen of the L.C.C. hospitals were ready for evacuation to hospitals 30 to 50 miles out of London, and by 1 October more than 16,000 beds would have been available for casualties in air raids.

Future plans for London's development include a £1,600,000 scheme for opening up a new embankment and riverside promenade on the south bank of the Thames between Westminster and Waterloo Bridges, so that there will be a riverside walk from County Hall to Waterloo Bridge with an open space 100 feet wide beside the river.

A new Thames tunnel, duplicating the Blackwall tunnel, is to be constructed at a cost of £2,824,000.

A further 2450 acres are to be added to London's Green Belt, including 68 acres at Boreham Wood, Hertfordshire, the High Elms estate at Farnborough, Kent, about 500 acres adjoining Enfield Chase and a further 500 acres at Chipstead. The L.C.C. are subscribing £100,000 towards this.

A further £1,000,000 has been voted for new buildings on a site of 64 acres in Stoke Newington, and an open belt of land 50 feet wide is to be laid out with seats, shrubs and grass verges to provide a promenade of about half a mile along the shores of two large lakes that are used as reservoirs of the Metropolitan Water Board. Houses will occupy 40 acres and part will be reserved for tennis courts, playgrounds, a community centre and a school.

One of the most necessary modern reforms is the construction of new routes out of London, and Sir Charles Bressey's committee has now issued a report of its recommendations which will enable the L.C.C. to go ahead with schemes for making transit through London easier for motor traffic.

On the whole, therefore, the L.C.C. may well congratulate itself on the work that it has achieved during the first fifty years of its life.

It has had to face terrific problems and these problems certainly do not grow less.

Modern warfare has infinitely increased the dangers of crowding into cities.

Modern legislation has been unable to rid us of unemployment.

Modern science has to struggle harder than ever to prevent disease and alleviate pain.

Modern education fights to secure equal intellectual opportunity for everybody.

But we have still a grim struggle ahead to secure prosperity and good health for all London's citizens.

All the more praise is therefore due to those men and women whose sense of public spirit is so highly developed that they will devote the greater part of their lives to the business of protecting London's citizens without any hope of reward, but the certainty of frequent blame.

People nearly always imagine local government to be something very mysterious and rather harsh.

The very mention of an Act of Parliament makes some people shy.

But Acts of Parliament, about which you will hear a lot in this book, don't bite. Indeed they are formed to see that you don't get bitten.

If you look round and see how very thoroughly the L.C.C. takes care of you, you may on your part decide that when the time comes you will take a helping hand in this organisation and not be willing just to be one of the helped.

Chapter 2   OTHER LONDON SERVICES

The City of London Corporation looks after the public health, highways, bridges and street improvements, open spaces, housing, and weights and measures of the City. It spends about £2½ millions a year, and covers an area of just over one square mile.

The Corporation consists of a Lord Mayor elected by the Court of Aldermen from the aldermen who have served the office of sheriff, upon the nomination of livery men of the City Companies in Common Hall. He holds office for one year. There are, in addition, twenty-five aldermen representing the twenty-five wards of the City and one for Bridge Ward Without. Aldermen are elected for life. There are also 206 common councillors, making 232 members in all.

The City has been responsible for the rebuilding of

Southwark Bridge, the London Fruit Exchange at Spital-fields, the disposal of refuse in the marshy ground of Hornchurch, and many rehousing schemes. It controls its own police force and maintains the Guildhall School of Music, the City of London Boys' and Girls' Schools and the City Freemen's School. It is responsible for inspecting all ships that enter the Port of London.

It was due to the efforts of the City authorities that over 2500 acres of common land were restored by them to Epping Forest. They then bought a further 3000 acres and became conservators of the whole area of 5600 acres. They have enlarged the Green Belt by giving Highgate Wood, Kilburn Park, Burnham Beeches, Coulsdon Common, Farthing Down, Kenley Common, Spring Park and West Wickham Common.

They have also opened a small open space in Bridge-water Square for workers in the offices and warehouses nearby.

The Metropolitan Borough Councils are composed of 1386 councillors and 227 aldermen from the boroughs of Battersea, Bermondsey, Bethnal Green, Camberwell, Chelsea, Deptford, Finsbury, Fulham, Greenwich, Hackney, Hammersmith, Hampstead, Holborn, Islington, Kensington, Lambeth, Lewisham, Paddington, Poplar, St Marylebone, St Pancras, Shoreditch, Southwark, Stepney, Stoke Newington, Wandsworth, Westminster (City) and Woolwich, of which the largest in size is Wandsworth, nearly 10,000 acres, with a population of nearly 400,000.

They spend over £16,000,000 a year.

You see from this how enormous is the work that they are called upon to do. They have also the thankless task of collecting all the rates, not only for services done by themselves but also for the L.C.C. and the Metropolitan Police.

The best way of realising what the Metropolitan Borough Councils do is to glance down their expenses' sheet and see how they spend this £16,000,000.

Electricity supply	£4,945,204
Street maintenance, repair and improvement	2,857,721
Housing and clearance	1,409,807
Removal and destruction of refuse	1,185,812
Establishment charges	1,161,288
Baths, wash-houses, and open bathing places	673,206
Street lighting	571,819
Maternity and child welfare	385,137
Public libraries, museums, etc.	332,704
Sewerage and drainage	311,549
Private street works (rechargeable)	239,244
Public conveniences	221,962
Salaries of sanitary officers, etc.	194,931
Rate collection	196,349
Parks and Open Spaces	184,394
Burial grounds	182,195
Infectious disease (notification and disinfection)	104,637
Treatment of tuberculosis	99,153
Registration of electors	63,852
Valuation	61,870
Registration of births, deaths and marriages	41,730
Other health services	26,295
Borough council elections	23,782
Sale of Food and Drugs Acts	22,912
Vaccination	17,432
Legal and Parliamentary expenses	16,874
Mortuaries and post-mortem rooms	15,896
Miscellaneous	456,738
	£16,004,493

Their duties are entirely distinct from those entrusted to the L.C.C., but they have also to share many duties with the L.C.C.

The L.C.C. sanctions street names and the boroughs put them up. The L.C.C. is the authority for the numbering of houses and its orders are carried into execution by the local bodies. The L.C.C. owns the tuberculosis sanatoria, but the Borough Councils are responsible for the tuberculosis clinics.

The L.C.C. owns the large open spaces, while all the smaller ones (under two acres) are owned by the Borough Councils.

The clearance of large insanitary areas under the Housing Act is carried out by the L.C.C. and of small areas by the Borough Councils.

Each Metropolitan borough is consulted about the general town and country planning which is the L.C.C.'s authority. The boroughs co-operate with the L.C.C. in securing better housing accommodation for the poorer people. Borough Councils are, however, bound to rehouse their displaced tenants within their own territory.

During the last twenty-five years the units of electricity sold in the County of London have risen from 70 millions to 770 millions.

There has been a fall in infant mortality in the last twenty-five years from 103 per thousand to 67. This decline is due to the work done by the boroughs in teaching mothers, preventing ill-health and in ensuring adequate food.

The boroughs have been responsible for traffic safety in putting up signs, signals and crossings.

The Metropolitan Water Board spends £5,000,000 a year. It consists of sixty-six members and it came into existence in 1903 as the result of the Metropolis Water Act. Before that time the water supply of London had been in the hands of eight independent water companies.

Its area covers 570 square miles. It supplies $7\frac{1}{4}$ million persons, who require 1,350,000 independent services to give an average rate per head of 40 gallons a day.

The record used in any one day is 374½ million gallons.

There are forty-nine storage reservoirs for unfiltered water and ninety-five service reservoirs for filtered water.

The head office of the M.W.B. in Rosebery Avenue stands partly on the site of the famous Round Pond of Sir Hugh Myddelton, who constructed the reservoir known as the New River Head to supply the City with water in 1603.

The Queen Mary reservoir at Littleton opened in 1925 contains 6750 million gallons of water and is the largest reservoir of its kind in the world. It can supply the whole of London for three weeks. It is actually larger than the City of London.

The London Passenger Transport Board, by virtue of the London Passenger Transport Act 1933, is the one coordinating authority for bus, tram, trolley bus, rail and coach services over an area of nearly 2000 square miles, serving a population of 9,400,000.

From ninety-two different companies there has now emerged a Board of seven members to control the largest urban transport organisation in the world, and operate vehicles over 227 miles of railway, 324 miles of tramway, 18 miles of trolley bus route and 2388 miles of roads. It owns 12,071 vehicles and 186 stations. It has a staff of 76,000 men and it is responsible for carrying about ten million passengers a day.

One of its most pleasing features is the artistic design of its stations and the colourfulness of its advertising campaign. It always gives the intending passenger the idea that any journey he takes by L.P.T.B. is an adventurous and beautiful holiday.

The Port of London Authority consists of twenty-eight members and spends £5,500,000 a year.

It exercises authority over an area from an imaginary straight line drawn from high-water mark on the bank of the Thames at the boundary between Teddington and

Twickenham to high-water mark on the opposite bank, extending down both sides of the Thames to an imaginary straight line drawn from the pilot mark at the entrance to Havengore Creek in Essex on a bearing 166° reckoned clockwise from the true north point of the compass to high-water mark on the Kent bank and including all islands, rivers, streams, creeks, waters, watercourses, channels, harbours and docks, that is, a distance of seventy miles.

Trinity House is responsible for pilotage, lighting and buoying, and the City of London is the health authority of the port.

The Thames Conservancy has relinquished its powers in this area.

The Port of London Authority has made the longest deep-water channel in the world, enabling vessels of fair burden to berth almost under the arches of London Bridge. By taking out 52 million tons of soil the P.L.A. has made the estuary easy for the pilots of even the largest ships; and all and every day you can see the dredgers still at work.

The wet docks under the control of the P.L.A. are St Katherine, London, Surrey, Surrey Canal, Millwall, King George V, Royal Albert and Tilbury. There is a floating, self-propelled crane which lifts 150 tons.

The King George V graving dock has a length of $750\frac{1}{4}$ feet, and New Tilbury graving dock is a couple of feet longer.

The total imports in a year are valued at more than £350,000,000 and the total exports at £112,000,000. Liverpool's export figures are rather higher, but her imports are about one-third of this.

The approximate annual traffic is 62 million tons of shipping and 43 million tons of goods.

The prosperity of the P.L.A. is due to the fact that it is a great distributing centre and is open to all producers and merchants from any part of the world without distinction.

Chapter 3   LONDON'S MONEY

The annual Budget of the L.C.C. comes to far more than the national Budget of certain countries, such as Denmark, Greece, Portugal or Turkey.

Roughly £67,000,000 is the amount expended each year on the day-to-day upkeep of local services in London.

It is met by fees, charges, rents and grants from Government, the balance being made up by the levy of a general rate, imposed by each borough in the form of so much in the £ on the annual value of the occupied fixed property in each borough, except that manufacturers' properties are rated at only one-quarter of their annual value.

So you see that the rate varies a good deal according to the borough.

In Poplar the rate rises to 18s. in the £ and in Westminster it is only 10s. 3d.

The average rate is 12s. 0½d., of which 8s. 0½d. goes to

the L.C.C., 1s. for the Police and 3s. 0¼d. for the local Borough Council.

The Borough Councils are responsible for keeping up the roads and pavements, street lighting, cemeteries, removal of refuse, public health and sanitary inspection, maternity and child welfare, covered-in baths and washhouses, public libraries, housing (to a limited extent) and certain air-raid precautions.

Some of the boroughs supply electricity and the City of London has its own Police Force and looks after certain bridges across the Thames.

Woolwich spends about £2,000,000 a year, and Stepney £1,400,000, which is a good deal more than the city of Bath spends.

In 1938–39 provision is made for the expenditure by the L.C.C. of about £53,000,000, of which £10,000,000 will go on land and permanent works and will mainly be met by borrowing: part is met from Road Fund grants and part is met by the rates. The remaining £43,000,000 is for day-to-day services and the way in which it is divided may be seen in the following table:

Education	£13,700,000
Public health (including hospitals)	7,700,000
Public assistance (relief of the destitute and mental hospitals)	6,300,000
Housing, including slum clearance	5,800,000
Bridges, highways, ferry and street improvements	1,200,000
Main sewers	1,100,000
Fire brigade	1,000,000
Parks	500,000
Capital expenditure to be met from revenue	1,000,000
Contingency provision (A.R.P. and so on)	800,000

The rest (about £4,000,000) goes towards the welfare of the blind, interest, regulative services and establishment expenses.

The bill is met as follows:

Rents, fees, contributions, interest, etc.	£8,500,000
Grants from Government	8,700,000
Drawn from surplus working balances	2,200,000
Rates	23,800,000

The Government grants relate mainly to education, housing and the General Exchequer grant, which represents the Council's share of a pool of money provided by the Government towards the general expenses of all local authorities and is divided up according to population, number of children under five, intensity of unemployment and sparsity of population. This peculiar formula is supposed to reflect the measure of relative need of Government assistance by individual local authorities.

The Council's capital expenditure of £10,000,000 goes mainly in housing, including slum clearance, street improvements and bridges, education, parks, hospitals, mental hospitals, main sewers, fire brigade, public assistance institutions and the extension of the County Hall.

Housing takes more than half this money, for the average cost of a single flat, including the site, is between £800 and £900, and as 10,000 new flats are the minimum aimed at by the L.C.C. every year you will soon see the reason for that.

The L.C.C. is allowed by law to borrow in the ordinary way of issuing stock or bonds.

At the present day its debt runs to £119,186,000, which sounds a tremendous lot, but it has pretty good security.

The L.C.C. was the first local authority in England to be given power to issue stock. The City of London and the Police have now similar powers, but the Metropolitan boroughs have not.

The L.C.C. is compelled by law to repay its capital

borrowings within maximum periods approved by the Treasury.

Generally speaking, the maximum time for land and bridges is sixty years, for buildings other than schools fifty years, for schools forty years. For housing the periods are somewhat longer.

The L.C.C. Budget is prepared annually after the summer holidays by the Department of the Comptroller getting into touch with all the spending departments regarding their requirements for the next year. These estimates are prepared in immense detail and compared with all past expenditures and tested in various other ways.

Each year cost-per-head tables are produced, and from these we discover that a patient in a L.C.C. general hospital costs from £3. 10s. 1d. to £5. 11s. 6d. per week according to the size and other circumstances of the hospital.

The 22,000 mental patients cost about 33s. 3d. a week each.

The cost of educating each London elementary school child is £22. 10s. a year. The secondary school education costs nearly £44 a year for each pupil.

The average cost of each of the ten thousand Fire Brigade calls each year is £90.

The average rent charged by the L.C.C. for its houses and flats is £27. 10s. a year, but receipts fall short of expenses by over £1,000,000, which works out at £13. 5s. a year each house and flat.

Chapter 4   LONDON'S SCHOOLS

The aim of the L.C.C. in education is to provide an open door for all London children so that they may be encouraged to avail themselves of the education best adapted to their needs.

As soon as a child reaches the age of ten and has enjoyed the privileges of the infant and junior schools, he or she is presented with a booklet, *Now you are ten*, showing what lies ahead.

First, there is the Secondary school, at which he is entitled to a special place if he does well enough in the Junior County Scholarships Examination.

If he fails to win a scholarship, he can try for one of 1250 local special places.

Even if he fails altogether, he can sit, at 13, for a supplementary Junior County Scholarship or go in the ordinary way as a fee-payer.

About 8000 children who do well in the Junior County Scholarships Examination but fail to get a scholarship are offered places in Central schools.

If the child does not go to either the Secondary or Central school, there still remains the Senior school.

At a Secondary school it is possible to stay until a boy or girl is 18 or 19, but a transfer can be effected at 13½ to a Junior Technical school.

At 16 or 17 the Secondary school pupil takes the General School Examination, the passing of which may excuse candidates from an entrance test to such professions as those of architect, chartered accountant, chemist, doctor, engineer, lawyer, surveyor or teacher. It also enables pupils who do well enough to pass into the University of London without taking the Matriculation Examination.

The Central school gives a four- or five-year course which is intended to fit a boy for industry or commerce. Facilities are given for learning bookkeeping, shorthand, typewriting and modern languages as well as woodwork and metalwork. Central schools are free.

In the Senior schools, in addition to woodwork and metalwork, drawing, painting, lettering, bookbinding and pottery are frequently taught. School journeys are sometimes undertaken, which may take the form of a fortnight's holiday in camp under the charge of a teacher. There are also school plays, concerts and debates.

From the Senior school the child is encouraged to go on to the day continuation school or evening institute.

From medieval days until the nineteenth century elementary education was mainly supplied by religious organisations. In 1833 Parliament voted £20,000 for public education, and this was the first of the grants that have been continued annually without interruption ever since.

It was administered by the Treasury and distributed by the National Society and the British and Foreign Schools Society.

In 1839 the grant was increased to £30,000 and its administration entrusted to a committee of the Privy Council known as the Education Department.

In 1870 came the famous "Forster" Act, by which School Boards were elected to supplement the number of schools and to support them from the rates.

So there were two types of school, the voluntary schools of the religious bodies and the Board schools of the publicly elected bodies. Each had help from the State, each charged fees.

In 1891 a further grant enabled education to be free, so in London all Board schools were made free, but some voluntary schools continued to charge a fee until 1905, in which year the L.C.C. abolished fees in all elementary schools.

Secondary schools had existed for centuries without State support, but in the nineteenth century the State began to aid higher education with grants and in 1889 local authorities were enabled to support technical education out of the rates.

At the close of the nineteenth century one State department controlled elementary education and another aided secondary education. The elementary voluntary schools were often short of funds; the Board schools, on the other hand, were maintained out of the rates.

In 1899 the State departments responsible for education were merged into the Board of Education, thus securing unity of State control.

Unity of local administration was secured by the "Balfour" Act of 1902, whereby the local education authority was made responsible for education of every

Above: London Schoolboys. Bermondsey 1894
Below: Bermondsey Schoolboys in 1934

School playgrounds—Junior (*above*) and Senior Elementary

kind, including the duty of maintaining the voluntary schools.

Then came, in 1906, the Education (Provision of Meals) Act enabling local education authorities to provide meals for children who needed them, an Act of 1907 which started a system of medical inspection, the Children Act of 1908 to look after neglected children, and the Mental Deficiency Act of 1913 which made provision for mentally defective children.

The third great Education Act, known as the "Fisher" Act (1918), remodelled the relations between central and local authorities, placing for the first time on each local education authority the responsibility of preparing its own scheme of education.

The Education Act 1921 simplified all educational legislation and is still the main source of reference for anyone who wants to know how education is controlled.

By the Local Government Act of 1929 Poor Law schools came under the L.C.C.

The main idea of the educational system to-day is to give each teacher the greatest possible freedom in their methods of teaching.

The State pays out of taxes about 37 per cent and the Council pays out of rates about 58 per cent of the total cost of education.

Nearly 788,000 pupils attend the schools, institutes and colleges of the L.C.C., 467,000 being under 14 years of age. They range in age from babies in nursery schools to very old grandfathers in evening schools.

There are fifty members of the L.C.C. Education Committee. The County is divided into twelve districts each of which is in charge of a divisional officer. There is also a principal organiser of children's care work, and there are five divisions for school medical work.

School supplies are obtained by the chief officer of supplies, who is responsible for the purchase and issue of the bulk of the stores.

Schools are visited by inspectors and organisers working under a chief inspector.

There is an Education Library in County Hall housing 60,000 volumes.

Ninety per cent of the children in London receiving full-time education attend the Elementary schools, which are either provided (Council) schools or non-provided voluntary schools. The same scale of salaries and the same regulations are in force in both types of schools.

The buildings vary much in age. The oldest are plain brick buildings with huge unwieldy classrooms. Then there are schools with large halls and large playgrounds built before the war, and to-day there is the severely simple style where everything is sacrificed to utility and comfort. The modern Elementary schools of one or two storeys are a delight to the eye both outside and in. The classrooms allow a generous space to each pupil and the windows open out on to playgrounds and let in the maximum of sunshine and fresh air.

The floors are of teak, the children work at tables, the walls are gay with colourful decorations, often designed by the children; and the infants have magnificent playrooms well equipped with every sort of toy.

It is compulsory for all children to attend school from the age of 5 until the end of the term in which they reach the age of 14. Children may be admitted at 3 and may stay until they are 16, though very few stay on after 14 except in Central schools.

There are four terms with $4\frac{1}{2}$ weeks' holiday in the summer and a fortnight at Christmas and Easter. Schools may also have not more than eleven half-holidays in each year.

A collection of over two million reading books is kept, from which schools may borrow to ensure a good supply of general reading matter.

The infant school stage is finished when the child is about $7\frac{3}{4}$. At this age the child has grappled with the "three R's" in the morning sessions and has enjoyed opportunities of more or less free expression in the afternoon.

The Junior school occupies all those between 8 and 11 and gives more scope for handwork, and a natural increasing development of English and arithmetic.

Those of the Junior school who are up to standard pass on into the Central and Secondary schools. The rest go on to the Senior schools, which provide encouragement for many types of talent not before brought out.

The traffic danger in London is so great that whenever circumstances permit, new schools are being built away from main roads, and pupils are escorted across the main thoroughfares.

So much care has been taken over "Safety First" for children, that whereas the increase in adult accidents has been alarming the accidents to children are decreasing steadily.

All boys receive instruction in handicrafts, and girls are taught domestic economy, which includes cookery, laundry, housewifery and infant care.

Physical education is compulsory, and games are becoming better organised and more and more popular, fares from and to the playing-fields during school hours being paid by the Council.

Local school sports associations have done much to organise and co-ordinate inter-school and inter-district contests.

Large sites have been acquired on the edge of the County on which the L.C.C. has built classrooms and equipped grounds for organised games. Pupils with teachers visit the grounds every school day and combine their school lessons with organised games on properly prepared pitches.

Swimming instruction is provided in various public baths and certificates are issued to children passing certain tests.

About three hundred schools have wireless sets, the licence fee and maintenance being paid for by the Council but not the cost of the apparatus.

Schools are allowed to "listen-in" to certain talks specially devised by the B.B.C. for schools.

A certain number of schools have private cinematograph installations and organised parties of children are occasionally taken to see public performances.

Visits are paid by the L.C.C. pupils to famous public buildings, art galleries, museums, the Zoo, the docks, and factories, the cost being borne by the Council.

One of the most successful enterprises sponsored by the School Journey Association and encouraged by the L.C.C. is the system of school journeys which started in 1896.

The aim is to illustrate school lessons in literature, history, civics and geography and to enable the children to do field-work in nature study, map-reading, drawing, and the like.

But in actual fact it has had far wider effects than this. It has brought teachers and pupils together and provided a grand opportunity for the child to improve its manners and social habits. Grants made by the Council for this purpose are supplemented by parents' contributions, school funds and private generosity.

At one elementary school, at Rotherhithe, free tuition is given to boys of 12 who wish to become sailors.

A Junior (Nautical) Day Technical school has been

Above: Mothercraft
Below: School Library

Above: The workshop of a Technical Institute
Below: The garden of a Girls' Secondary School

opened at the L.C.C. school for Engineering and Navigation, Poplar, for training boys at 14 years old.

Children are encouraged in Elementary schools to do home lessons, which are not however enforced against the wishes of the parents. These lessons are sometimes prepared in the schools, and quiet reading in evening libraries is also popular with both children and parents.

Quite a number of schools have flourishing botanical classes, and practical work is done in school gardens.

Music is popular in all schools.

The experiment of encouraging parents and friends to see the children at work by holding frequent open days has proved very successful.

The Central schools are a development of the Higher Grade schools established in 1898.

They came into being in 1911 and have a definite bias, either commercial or technical. There is a general education for two years and then a bias is introduced either with a commercial or an industrial career in view.

Pupils are selected for transfer at the age of 11 and expected to stay for four years.

The Secondary schools were in many cases very ancient foundations established by private benefactors, and these took grants from the Council. A good number of the maintained Secondary schools have had to be specially built. About 60 per cent of the pupils in Secondary schools are admitted free or at reduced fees. The fees vary from £4. 10s. to sixty guineas a year, and the curriculum aims at pupils of 16 being able to pass the General School Examination. An increasing number of pupils stay on to take the Higher School Examination at 17 or 18.

The Council also gives grants to the University of London.

Four colleges for the training of teachers are maintained by the L.C.C.: Avery Hill, Eltham, Furzedown (Streatham) for women students, and Shoreditch Technical Institute for men in handicraft work.

Three other colleges for training teachers in special subjects are aided by the Council: the National Training School of Cookery, Westminster, where you can get one of the best luncheons in London, the Domestic Science Department of the Battersea Polytechnic, and the Chelsea College of Physical Training at the Chelsea Polytechnic.

Refresher courses for teachers are held at the L.C.C. College of Physical Education in Paddington Street, St Marylebone. In various other centres lectures and classes for teachers are organised every year to enable them to keep in touch with all modern developments in educational theory and practice.

The first stage in scholarships is that for the 10 or 11 year olds. The scholarships enable successful candidates to proceed to Secondary schools on the results of an examination in English, Arithmetic and General Knowledge, but there are also supplementary scholarships awarded at 13, trade scholarships at the same age, intermediate scholarships for those between 16 and 18, Senior County scholarships at 18 available at Universities, teachers' scholarships and special talent scholarships for special talent in drawing, painting and music.

The L.C.C. provides every opportunity for continued education.

Early in the nineteenth century there were founded a good many night schools, mechanics' institutes, and working-men's colleges. In the night schools, the illiterate could learn the "three R's". The mechanics' institutes provided scientific and technical instruction to workmen. The working-men's colleges trained working men to understand social and economic problems.

The modern evening institute is the outcome of the old night school. The mechanics' institute has developed into the technical institute and the working-men's colleges inspired the University Extension Movement, the W.E.A. Educational Settlements and other forms of adult education.

From 1873 to 1904 the School Board for London kept going, with a hiatus of seven years, the continuation schools, and from 1893 to 1904 the L.C.C. conducted a number of technical institutes.

In 1904 the L.C.C., having taken over the duties of the School Board, developed a complete scheme for the London area.

The Polytechnics, which provide day and evening education both for manual and professional workers, owe much to Quintin Hogg, who desired to link technical education with social, spiritual and recreational activities. They all cater for women as well as for men. One of them, the City of London College, is concerned with commercial education and the technology of commodities.

There is a School of Building at Brixton, a School of Printing and Kindred Trades, a School of Photo-engraving, at Shoreditch Technical Institute the furniture trade is taught, at the Cordwainers' Technical Institute boot and shoe manufacture is undertaken, while the Leathersellers' Company's Technical College specialises in dyeing and dressing leather.

There are fourteen schools of art maintained or aided by the L.C.C., the fine arts being taught at the Chelsea, Westminster, and Regent Street Polytechnics, and the arts and handicrafts at the Central School of Arts and Crafts and the Camberwell and Hammersmith Schools.

In the trade schools, which offer specialised training for those who want to become skilled workers, courses are given in engineering, building, navigation, carriage and motor-body building, cabinet-making, silversmithing, printing, bookbinding, photo-engraving, professional cookery, professional waiting, tailoring, hairdressing, the meat trade, rubber trade and boot and shoemaking.

For girls there are courses in dressmaking, tailoring, millinery, upholstery, photography, hairdressing, and domestic occupations.

These schools keep in close touch with the leading firms, in order that all their pupils may find suitable work.

There are twelve voluntary day continuation schools where London boys and girls from 14 to 18 may attend for a minimum of 6 and a maximum of 15 hours a week and gain preliminary training for commercial and industrial careers.

The evening institutes are broadly divided into those for Juniors, that is those under 18, and those for Seniors, those over 18. The fees charged are quite small and for those who are very poor there are no fees.

There are twenty-one Senior commercial institutes with courses in accountancy, banking, shipping, insurance, law, local government, auctioneering and estate agency, and secretarial work. Modern languages are taught and short-hand and typewriting and bookkeeping.

The Junior commercial institutes provide a two-year preliminary training for the Seniors that is mainly vocational, but also provides physical exercises and aesthetics.

Attached to the polytechnics and technical institutes there are also Junior technical institutes providing specialised training in particular trades.

Literary institutes are designed for adults who desire a cultural education. So, literature, philosophy, elocution, drama, history, art, appreciation of architecture, and music also have a place in the curriculum.

The men's institutes provide recreation activities for those who wish to develop hobbies. Their success has been remarkable, due perhaps to the degree of self-government they have attained. Junior men's institutes are run on similar lines for boys between 14 and 18.

Women's institutes for all girls and women over 14 give instruction in dressmaking, cookery, needlework, domestic crafts, in health subjects, and in a wide range of recreation arts.

Special training is provided for the blind at the Royal School, Leatherhead, the Royal Normal College, Norwood, the Blind Employment Factory in Waterloo Road, and other places, where they are taught basketry, brush and matmaking, chair-caning, book-repairing, piano-tuning, weaving, machine knitting, and shorthand and typewriting.

A particularly notable advance has been made in child welfare.

Every child in the L.C.C. schools is medically examined on entering the school, at the age of 7, at 11, and in the last term but one.

School nurses examine all the children in all schools every term at least once, and school dentists also inspect them every year of school life.

There are eighty-one centres and eighteen hospitals where children are treated for, tonsils, adenoids, teeth, ringworm and diseases of the skin, eyes and ears.

There are also curative centres for stammerers.

Twelve district organisers supervise the work of voluntary workers on school care committees, who advise parents on medical treatment, assess charges to parents for meals and medical treatment, and help to find suitable employment for the children.

Other voluntary workers undertake the after care of

children leaving schools for the blind, deaf and physically defective.

Meals, including milk and cod liver oil and malt, are provided in the schools, and dinners are prepared for those who through lack of food are unable to benefit from education. The law demands that parents pay full or part cost of these meals according to their means.

London play-centres owe their initiation to Mrs Humphry Ward, who for twelve years carried them on by her own efforts.

Over half of the Foundling Hospital site has been bought partly by Lord Rothermere and partly by the public to secure a play-centre in the heart of London.

The L.C.C. looks after three nursery schools and makes grants to nineteen others.

These schools are open to children of two years old and they leave at five.

They are much more like nurseries than schools and provide a magnificent opportunity for quiet rest, healthy and safe exercise, reasonable meals and good companionship.

There are 9500 children in the London "special" schools for the defective; a further 2500 delicate children, including those disposed to tuberculosis, attend day open-air schools, and 4000 delicate children are sent for short periods to residential open-air schools.

There are two junior day schools for the blind, and at 13 they are transferred to residential schools till they are 16.

There are six junior day schools for the deaf, and they too are transferred at 13 to residential schools till they are 16.

The compulsory school age for the mentally defective is from 7 to 16. About half the time is given up to manual occupations.

The physically defectives are usually crippled or afflicted with weak hearts.

A fleet of seventy-two L.C.C. motor ambulances takes children who are unable to travel in public vehicles to and from school.

The first open-air school was opened in Woolwich in 1907, and there are now fifteen, nine for anaemic children and six for children inclined to tuberculosis.

There are three residential open-air schools, one at Bushey Park for boys, and for girls one at Margate and one at St Leonards. Children are sent to these schools for four or six weeks.

There are 3000 children accommodated in the special children's hospitals and teaching is provided for about 2000 of them.

Delinquents are sent to approved schools, the type of school varying according to the age of the young offender.

The L.C.C. maintains five approved schools, three for boys (Mayford, Mile Oak and Ardale) and two for girls (Gisburne House and Cumberland Lodge). There are about 1300 London children in L.C.C. and other approved schools.

A further 5500 destitute children are maintained and educated by the L.C.C.

There are five boarding schools where they receive ordinary elementary education until they are 15 and are taught bakery, painting, tailoring, shoemaking and the rest. There are also three homes where children are boarded and go out to ordinary elementary schools.

Some of these schools are large barrack-like places, others are large cottages holding from sixteen to sixty children under the care of foster-fathers and foster-mothers.

Two hundred and fifty boys between 12 and 16 are

trained for sea life in the training ship *Exmouth*, which lies in the Thames off Grays.

If you look at the way the L.C.C. spends its money you may be surprised to see what a huge amount seems to go on education, well over one-third of the total spent on all services.

You may then equally wonder why so large a proportion of London's children appear to need the more expensive attention of special schools to cope with their physical, mental and moral disabilities.

It really is just another example to show you how the main function of the L.C.C. is to protect and care for its citizens.

The process of raising the general level of health and intellectual vigour is slower than any of us like, but a quick glance at the past shows us that the general level is being raised. We are not falling back.

The health standard, owing in great part to Sir George Newman, is now so infinitely better than it was at the beginning of the century that on that count alone the money devoted to educational services could be called well spent.

But education has played its part in encouraging national thrift to such an extent that National savings have risen from £285 millions in 1913 to £1336 millions in 1936.

As a result of education London's citizens lead far healthier lives and take far more interest in outside affairs.

The vulgar and sensational in film and newspaper still exerts a much stronger hold on the public than educational reformers like, but there has been a steady increase in the numbers of readers in public libraries and a distinct advance in liberal thought.

Most noticeable of all has been the change for the better in the manners and appearance of the young.

Boys and girls both take infinitely more pride in their personal appearance than they did forty years ago. There is far more self-respect and far less servility on the one hand or rudeness on the other than there was at the beginning of the century.

Many things have combined to produce these happy effects, but certainly education has led the way, and the result of better paid teachers, smaller classrooms, more light and air, and a liberally conceived programme of subjects has been a vastly improved type of boy and girl.

It shows how highly the L.C.C. value education that they are willing to spend more than £14,000,000 on it annually.

When you consider that half a million children benefit from elementary education and a quarter of a million students are gaining a higher education you may agree that the figure is not too high.

Chapter 5   LONDON'S HOUSES

The housing problem is one of the most acute of modern times, but it is not new.

In an Act of Parliament dated 1593 we read:

"Great mischiefs daily grow and increase by reason of pestering the houses with divers families, harbouring of inmates, and converting great houses into several tenements, and the erection of new buildings in London and Westminster."

And in Charles I's reign we are told that:

"The City is so compassed in and straightened with these new buildings that it may prove very dangerous to the inhabitants."

The Great Fire of 1666 cleared 13,200 dwelling-houses, covering an area of 436 acres, occupying 400 streets.

Unfortunately Sir Christopher Wren's plan for reconstruction was only partially carried out and the overcrowding began again.

The beginning of the nineteenth century saw a tremendous expansion of industrial development and houses were built quickly and badly. There were no building laws to regulate the buildings, so the largest number of people were crammed into the smallest possible area and London in consequence grew, as I said before, like Topsy, anyhow.

In a report to the Poor Law Commissioners of 1838 we read of:

"Quarters inhabited by hundreds of thousands of the labouring classes...crowding more or less dense in courts and alleys and narrow streets almost insusceptible of ventilation, in dwellings which themselves were often not fit to be inhabited by human beings: while all around the dwellings the utter absence of drainage, the utter omission of scavenging and nuisance prevention, the utter insufficiency of water supply, conduced to such accumulations of animal and vegetable refuse, and to such pondings of ordurous liquids, as made one universal atmosphere of filth and stink."

And here is Charles Kingsley's picture of a Bermondsey slum in the middle of the nineteenth century. The passage is taken from *Alton Locke*:

"A miserable blind alley, where a dirty gas lamp just served to make darkness visible, and show the patched windows and rickety doorways of the crazy houses, whose upper storeys were lost in a brooding cloud of fog; and the pools of stagnant water at our feet; and the huge heap of cinders which filled up the waste end of the alley on a dreary, black formless mound on which two or three spectral dogs prowled up and down after the offal, appearing and vanishing like dark imps in and out of the black misty chaos beyond."

And, in passing, I may say that I have seen far worse than that recently, where in addition to these horrors, the kitchen has been ankle deep in water, the walls running with damp, the plaster come away, the floor boards broken and the roof leaking.

The first Public Health Act was passed in 1848, but housing legislation dates from 1851, when Lord Shaftesbury induced Parliament to pass the Common Lodging Houses Act and Labouring Classes Lodging Houses Act which secured the provision and inspection of lodging-houses.

Two more Acts, known as the Torrens Acts, enabled individual insanitary houses to be dealt with, and the Cross Acts of 1875 and 1879 enabled local authorities to clear and reconstruct unhealthy areas.

Two Housing of the Working Classes Acts 1885 and 1890 conferred on local authorities the power to carry out improvement schemes, to deal with small unhealthy areas, and to build new houses for the working classes.

Further Housing Acts led to the Town Planning Act of 1909, which introduced for the first time powers relating to the town planning of land.

Under the regime of the Metropolitan Board of Works (1855–89) sixteen clearance schemes resulted in the displacement of 22,872 people and provision for 27,730 people. The Board did not itself build houses. Six other schemes, involving the displacement of a further 6132 people, were begun by the Board and completed by the L.C.C., which took over in 1889.

One of the first steps of the Council was to create the office of Medical Officer of Health of the County of London, and some two hundred insanitary areas were inspected.

It then finished the work begun by the Board and began thirteen further clearance schemes, involving a displacement of 16,434 people.

Accommodation was provided for over 12,000 people

Sidney Street slum

Rebuilding London—Lambeth Bridge old and new

displaced owing to the construction of Thames bridges and tunnels and street widenings.

Three lodging-houses for men, accommodating nearly 2000, were also built. These were really a kind of working-man's hotel. Facilities were provided for the men to cook their own food if they wished.

Between 1899 and 1903, 300 acres of land on the outskirts of London were bought for the erection of cottage dwellings, and additional housing accommodation for 20,000 was provided by 1912.

By the time the war came in 1914 nearly 10,000 houses and flats had been provided at a cost of just over £3,000,000.

During the war no houses were built, and immediately after the war building was no longer profitable, and Addison's Act of 1919 recognised for the first time the principle of State subsidy for housing.

The assisted schemes under later acts provided for a State contribution of a fixed annual sum per house, the rest of the loss being borne by the rates.

In 1919 the Council started a five years' scheme for the erection of 29,000 houses to accommodate 145,000 people. Not all these were built. In addition 9447 were built under the 1919 Act and 6521 under the 1923 Act. Nearly 40,000 houses were provided between 1924 and 1934, under the Act of 1924, when this particular form of State grant ended.

The five-year plan of 1930, involving an expenditure of £21,825,000 on the provision of 34,670 houses and flats, could not be carried out owing to lack of money, but construction went on at two of the Council's cottage estates, Becontree and St Helier, and two fresh sites were acquired: 244 acres at Mottingham for £63,361, and 142 acres at Chigwell for £24,655.

In 1931 the Council considered the provision of small

houses specially suited to the aged and approved flats in two-storey buildings on cottage estates with stairs of less than normal rise.

In 1933 a further attempt was made to clear the slums and lists prepared of unhealthy areas classified under three heads:

(1) Small groups of houses in mews, courts and alleys where housing on the site was impracticable.

(2) Larger areas capable of redevelopment by erection of working-class houses.

(3) Groups of well-built houses overcrowded and in a bad state of repair.

A ten-year plan was drawn up involving the displacement of 250,000 people at a cost of £35,000,000.

In 1934 the Council adopted a programme for the beginning of operations in all large unhealthy areas during the three years June 1934 to June 1937.

A great deal of preliminary work has to be done, and so strict time and progress schedules have to be laid down for the building work. In order to increase the efforts of the Council's Architects Department architects in private practice have been employed to undertake the development of certain sites. Three estates have already been developed in this way, and proposals for the development of eleven further sites are being prepared by private architects.

In 1937, 7502 dwellings were provided, and it is even suggested that London's slum problem, except so far as the East End boroughs are concerned, may well be solved within the next ten years if the present rate of clearance and building goes on.

Up to 1937, £52,500,000 had been spent on the dwellings and estates.

Slums bring on pneumonia and pulmonary tuberculosis, and the lack of sunlight and air lowers the resistance of the body to these and other diseases, while the dampness so common in slums brings on catarrh and rheumatism. Privacy and cleanliness being impossible, both moral and physical degeneration follow.

There are four types of insanitary houses suitable for "clearance area" action:

(1) The two-storey terrace-type house built in the early nineteenth century in depressing standardised rows, separated at the back from other rows of identical houses by little shut-in yards. Inside there are usually four rooms with a lean-to washhouse, dark passage, dark, narrow, steep stairs, with damp walls and floors and leaking roof. Often the only chance of washing is under the tap in the yard. They are also frequently verminous. The only remedy for this sort of house is demolition and clearance.

(2) Cottages which once stood in semi-rural surroundings whose once long gardens have been snapped up by builders so that they now are so hemmed in as to have no light and little air. The street door opens into the living room and stairs lead from this room to the bedroom. Both rooms are low with small windows and damp, and vermin alone flourish. Here again demolition is the only remedy.

(3) The tenement, of three storeys and a basement, originally built for one family and now occupied by a different family in each room reduced to sharing one water-closet and one tap. These are often soundly built and present a great difficulty.

(4) The insanitary mews dwelling, built originally as stables, without ventilation or light in the back, with hay lofts and harness rooms above. Access is usually through a narrow passage and the buildings are grouped round a badly paved courtyard filled with costers' barrows, carts and cars. The living quarters are approached by steep stairs and often consist of the loft partitioned off into many

rooms. The back rooms are lit only by a skylight and the air is often stagnant.

One's first feeling is nearly always a strong desire to bomb the whole lot out of existence, but the problem is not capable of so easy a solution as that.

It often, indeed, takes two years or more between representation of the clearance area and its replacement by a new estate.

The responsibility for the change lies in the hands of the Valuer to the L.C.C., with the help of the Medical Officer of Health, the Solicitor and the Architect.

The local authority can deal with the cleaning up of an insanitary area either by means of a compulsory purchase order or by means of a clearance order.

In the first case the authority acquires the property, demolishes the buildings and itself redevelops the site. In the second the owners have to demolish the property.

The initial proceedings are rather intricate and formidable. The Valuer first indicates to the M.O.H. the available new housing, the M.O.H. indicates to the Valuer the area to be cleared, the Valuer then takes a census of rents, occupations, and prepares a survey plan.

The proposal is submitted to the Council and the Solicitor drafts the order, which is advertised in the press, and then submitted to the Ministry of Health for confirmation. There may even be a Public Inquiry. This all takes a considerable time, but as the Housing Report says: "Human beings cannot be moved like pawns on a chess board." Each individual case has to be considered on its own merits.

There is, furthermore, the legal aspect of the rights of property which still further complicates the negotiations.

Since the passing of the Housing Act 1930 up to the end of 1936 the Council had declared 165 areas to be clearance

Whitmore Estate: before clearance (*left*). To-day—Rover House (*right*)

Modern block dwellings: Clapham Park Estate (*above*),
and Oaklands Estate (*below*)

areas, 107 of them being dealt with by compulsory purchase and 58 by clearance orders. This involved an acreage of 306 acres and a population of 68,000 people.

Then comes the new procedure of "redevelopment". The utilisation of 20½ acres of Hackney Marsh made it possible to envisage a scheme of large-scale redevelopment, and it was decided to redevelop 46 acres in the northern part of Bethnal Green, where 583 houses are already condemned as unfit for human habitation, and nearly 50 per cent of the houses in the area and more are overcrowded. The redevelopment will involve the rehousing of 4700 people at a cost of £1,750,000.

Prior to 1935 overcrowding usually meant "more than two persons per room". There were in 1931 well over half a million people in London coming under this category. There are over 2000 people living more than seven persons per room. The Housing Act 1935 laid down a new standard for overcrowding, taking into account the number and size of the rooms in each dwelling, and it provided for a survey to ascertain what families were overcrowded and how many additional dwellings would be required to abate the overcrowding disclosed. Children under one year are not counted, and between one and ten count as half a person. In order to abate the overcrowding a total of 23,780 dwellings are required.

The new accommodation for the abatement of overcrowding may be provided either in block dwellings or houses.

Owing to the expense of building sites the accommodation usually takes the form of block dwellings, usually five storeys high, of self-contained flats with balcony access approached by common staircases. All rooms are 8 ft. 6 in. high and the average areas of the living rooms are from 150 to 160 sq. ft., while the areas of the bedrooms vary from 100 to 120 sq. ft. An entrance lobby leads to the living room and there are one, two, three or four bedrooms according to the tenants' requirements, a kitchen, a bathroom, and a water-closet.

There are four types of flats now in general use, some with coppers, some with wash-houses. Every living room has a coal fire, and one bedroom in every flat has a coal fire and a point for a gas fire. In other bedrooms there are plugs for electric fires.

Some of the flats on newer developments have staircase access as opposed to balcony access, dust-chutes to each staircase, with double entrance doors on the foot of each stairway leading into a roomy vestibule, and in more than two-room flats there is a private balcony outside the kitchen. Water-closets (except in one- and two-room flats) occupy separate compartments next door to and no longer in the bathroom.

These blocks of flats are so arranged that there is always a large open space as well as a completely equipped children's playground. Trees and shrubs are planted in the courtyards, and where possible existing trees have been carefully preserved.

Day-nurseries, maternity, child-welfare and community centres are being developed, and every fresh block of flats that goes up shows fresh improvements.

To get some idea of the revolution that is taking place in London's housing you should visit on the same day some of the old streets south of the Mile End Road and then go quickly to the King's Mead estate on Hackney Marsh, where you will see light and airy flats with soundproof rooms, sliding-doors separating dining room from parlour, the very latest labour-saving devices, any amount of cupboard space let into the walls, and so constructed as to ensure the maximum of sunlight flooding every room.

There is a large games area and a school on the estate and an open-air school on the other side of Homerton Road on Hackney Marsh.

The rents are of course proportionately higher for flats of this special type, a five-room flat coming to 22s. 6d. a week.

If you look carefully as you go through the streets of London you will see more and more of these handsomely built brick blocks of flats that the L.C.C. have substituted for the old unhealthy type of houses which the workman was condemned to endure.

The other method adopted by the L.C.C. to house its workers has been the creation of cottage estates.

So far as possible all the amenities of country life are preserved and encouraged.

Greens and shrubberies are cultivated at corners and little privet hedges maintained by the L.C.C. form a border to each cottage garden.

These cottages are of two or three storeys, the three-storey houses being used as flats of three or four rooms and the two-storey houses kept as houses of from three to five rooms, in addition to a kitchenette with deep sink, draining board, gas cooker, washing copper and shelving, bath, water-closet, larder, dresser cupboard and coal hole.

Parts of the estate are reserved for shops, schools, open spaces, churches and places of amusement.

As it takes a great deal of time to arrange with local authorities about gas, light, water and sewerage and so on, and involves a good deal of complicated calculation in contracting under fluctuating conditions, the Council worked out what is called a "value-cost" contract which has proved very valuable in speeding up the work.

The L.C.C. finances the undertaking and bears the cost of the work, one master-contractor being engaged for each estate and paid by a fee for his services on the following basis:

The contractor's fee is computed on the measured value of the work and is increased or decreased on a definite percentage scale according as to whether the actual cost is less or greater than the measured value.

There is a cottage estate at Roehampton, on land which was originally a private park, with a mansion that has been converted into a club house for the tenants with tennis courts adjoining. There are also $9\frac{1}{2}$ acres of allotments and a wooded land of $3\frac{1}{2}$ acres preserved as a children's recreation ground.

There are 1212 houses on this estate.

At Bellingham in Lewisham there are more than twice that number of houses, while at Downham there are 6054 houses, eight elementary schools, a central school, an open-air school, and a site reserved for a secondary school. Downham was built under a "value-cost" contract for £3,728,870. But the largest of these cottage estates by far is Becontree, which is the largest municipal housing estate in the world. It has an area of 2770 acres or more than four square miles. And it was bought when land was on the average about £250 an acre.

It lies about ten miles from Charing Cross, and when it was first built there was a fear lest it might be too far from the work place of many of its inhabitants, but the factories have gone out to Becontree; the great Ford works at Dagenham are within easy reach, so that fear was quickly driven away. In fact about one-third of the wage-earners on this estate are locally employed and have little or nothing to pay to get to and from their work.

Over 500 acres have been reserved for open spaces, including the large central open space of Parsloes Park, which possesses a magnificent cricket ground, bowling greens and a deep ornamental lake which has become a favourite haunt of wild duck.

Unless you actually go down to see it, it is extremely difficult to visualise the magnitude of the undertaking that is Becontree.

It occupies an area more than four times that of the City of London.

Its population of 120,000 is larger than that of Bournemouth or Preston and nearly as large as that of the City of Westminster.

It was formerly part of the forest of Essex, in Norman times a wild land of woods and heaths, marshes and grasslands.

As lately as three hundred years ago it was prized by the King above all his other forests.

It was disafforested in the middle of the nineteenth century and used for market-garden and farming purposes.

It was acquired for housing by the L.C.C. in 1919 and building began in 1920.

It is roughly circular and the roads have been named to perpetuate local historical associations.

There is a large open belt on the west and south reserved to insulate the estate from future surrounding development.

In addition to Parsloes Park, the manor house and grounds of Valence have been retained, and other parks adjacent include Goodmayes, Goresbrook, Central Park, Becontree Heath and Old Dagenham Park.

So there is no lack of facilities for getting into the open.

And over the flats you can see the tall red sails of the Thames barges on their way up and down the estuary.

The rents at Becontree vary from 5s. 7d. a week for one-room flats, 8s. 9d. a week for two-room flats, to

23s. 6d. a week for six-room cottages. There are many houses and flats at varying rents between those limits.

Every cottage and flat has a garden, front and back.

There are some thirty schools, as well as public libraries, swimming pools and the usual cinemas and inns. There is also a large number of aesthetic, social, religious, political, athletic and other organisations to draw people of similar interests into groups.

Electric trains and nine different bus services connect Becontree with London, the centre of which can be reached in about half an hour.

The total cost of building Becontree was about £14,000,000, and the work took fourteen years.

The result, whether seen from afar over the fields of the clean red-brick city of low buildings, or near over the spotless sunny avenues and gardens, is wholly delightful.

It is an undertaking that may well make the L.C.C. proud of its splendid foresight and vision.

It is planning new cottage estates all the time.

I have recently seen the beginnings of a new estate on the edge of Epping Forest at Chingford, where the rents run from 9s. 9d. for two rooms to 18s. 8d. for a five-room house. This estate will eventually comprise over 1500 dwellings, whose fortunate occupants will be able to roam at will over the pleasant glades and footpaths of the forest.

There is the Watling estate, for example, of 386 acres just north of the London aerodrome in Hendon. This estate, which is well wooded with a stream running through it, is completely self-contained, with its own schools, shops, churches, sports grounds and open spaces. There are over 4000 dwelling-houses erected at a cost of £2,285,000.

And close by is Kenmore Park. Also north of the Thames are the White Hart Lane estate of 138 acres and 2230 houses at Tottenham and Wood Green and the Chigwell estate near Hainault Forest.

On the west are Hanwell, with about 1500 houses, and Wormholt at Shepherd's Bush, of 68 acres and 895 houses. Nearby is the Old Oak estate consisting of 1056 houses.

The biggest estate south of the Thames is St Helier, which covers 825 acres and provides 9068 houses in the Merton and Morden areas. The new streets have been named after Abbeys in England and Wales as a reminder of the ancient Priory here. The cost of this estate was £4,078,500, and its population is about 40,000.

Smaller estates lie to the north of it at Totterdown Fields and Norbury.

South-east there are the four estates of Bellingham, Whitefoot Lane, Downham and Mottingham all close together.

Mottingham has preserved two woods and is admirably laid out in crescents, squares and avenues with the shopping facilities all grouped in the centre.

Bellingham has about 2670 houses, Whitefoot Lane over 1000; Downham, which occupies 522 acres, has 6058 houses and Mottingham has about 2000 houses.

There are in all twenty cottage estates and about 200 developments comprising block dwellings, and further sites are in course of acquisition.

The City of London has its own housing schemes, including one at Ilford, while the Metropolitan Borough Councils also build five-storey blocks of dwellings. Woolwich has developed large cottage estates of 334 acres at Eltham and 376 acres at Middle Park. Camberwell, Deptford, Greenwich, Lewisham and Wandsworth have also developed cottage estates.

There are also five philanthropic Trusts operating in London for Housing, the Peabody, Guinness, Sutton,

Samuel Lewis and Aubrey. The Aubrey Trust at Orchard House, Hammersmith, caters also for the social life of its tenants by the provision of two community centres and a girls' hostel. There are also some extremely attractive blocks in Kennington erected at the instigation of his former majesty King Edward VIII on the London estate of the Duchy of Cornwall.

The lowest rent for two rooms on block-dwelling estates is 4s. 6d. a week at Provost, the highest 15s. 11d. at Ossulston. The lowest rent for five rooms in block-dwelling estates is 13s. 4d. at Hughes Fields, the highest 25s. 7d. at Ossulston.

The lowest rent for two rooms on the cottage estates is 6s. 9d. at Old Oak, the highest 15s. 8d. at Roehampton. The lowest rent for five rooms is 13s. 5d. at White Hart Lane, the highest 29s. 1d. at Roehampton.

The average number of persons per dwelling over all estates is 4·4. The average number of persons per room is 1·43 in block dwellings and 1·21 in cottages.

Some idea of the size of the Council's housing operations may be gathered from the fact that it has provided up to the present time over 90,000 dwellings with an annual rent-roll of about £3,250,000. The departments chiefly concerned with the provision and subsequent management of these properties are the Architect's and the Valuer's. As I have mentioned above, the Council's Valuer is called upon to perform an immense amount of work in connection with slum clearance before actual clearance can take place. When the order has been confirmed he negotiates for the acquisition of the properties and eventually arranges for the removal of the families to be displaced and the demolition of the insanitary dwellings. The cleared site is then handed over for development in accordance with the scheme prepared by the Architect

after consultation with the Valuer. After redevelopment
the site is handed back to the permanent care of the
Valuer. In addition to the clearance-area sites other
land must be obtained for housing schemes, and the acquisition of the necessary sites is also a matter for the
Valuer.

It will be realised that the letting, management and
maintenance of these 90,000 properties is a tremendous
task. In the last year nearly 250,000 persons made
oral or written enquiries at the head office as to the
possibility of obtaining accommodation. The repairs and
maintenance of the dwellings and the upkeep of gardens,
greens and open spaces alone cost roughly £500,000 a
year, and a staff of nearly 3000 workmen is regularly
employed on this work. The task is constantly growing,
not only owing to the steady increase in the number of
properties but also because the word "management" is
interpreted in a liberal sense. Children's playgrounds and
community centres have already been provided on many
estates, and as each year passes new measures for the
comfort and well-being of the tenants are adopted. The
Council's efforts are not confined simply to moving families
from bad dwellings to good ones, but every endeavour is
made to ensure that the families will derive the greatest
possible benefit from the change. There are, of course, a
few families who fail to make a full response to their new
surroundings, but even in these cases there is a gain to be
found in the effect of better surroundings on the children.
So far as many of the tenants are concerned, the immediate
step of removal is not an isolated fact, but the beginning
of a system of social education which inculcates the virtues
of good citizenship.

Of all the Metropolitan boroughs Lambeth has supplied
the greatest number of tenants to the L.C.C. estates during

the last seven years, closely followed by Southwark, Poplar and Camberwell.

The chief occupation followed by L.C.C. tenants is that of labourer, 9798 having that occupation; while the second highest figure is that of 3282 motor-drivers.

The great majority of the tenants are those who belong to the lower-paid occupations, and in fact it is the policy of the L.C.C. to give preference in the letting of its dwellings to the lower-paid workers living in unsatisfactory conditions.

Prizes are given by the L.C.C. on the various cottage estates for the best front garden.

Houses on the street—old and new plan: Essex Street,
Hoxton (*above*), Roehampton Estate (*below*)

An Epping Forest glade

Chapter 6   LONDON'S GREENS

Parks and Open Spaces

There are few things that the average Londoner longs for
more than a sight of green fields, colourful flowers, and
the smell of good fresh air. There are few things more
necessary to his general well being.

In this respect, as in every other, his needs are most
carefully catered for by the L.C.C.

It is, as you can imagine, a problem of great difficulty
in an area already so congested to distribute the open
spaces as evenly or as widely as could be wished, but it is
possible to take a walk of some miles in London and to be
in the presence of trees and grass nearly all the way.

One of the most quickly informative and illuminating
series of maps ever produced by the Ordnance Survey
Office is that known (but nothing like well enough known)
as the Land Utilisation Series.

This shows you at once what proportion of the land is forest and woodland, meadowland and permanent grass, arable, heathland, moorland commons and rough pasture, gardens, allotments, orchards and nurseries, and what proportion is agriculturally unproductive.

Most of the best known parks in London were once Royal Hunting parks that were ultimately bequeathed by the Sovereigns to their people and are now regulated by the Government.

These are Richmond Park, Bushy, Hampton Court, Regent's Park, Hyde Park, Kew, Kensington, Greenwich, Woolwich, St James's Park, Old Deer Park, Richmond, Home Park Recreation Ground, Windsor, Primrose Hill and Green Park.

I have arranged them in order of size.

St James's Park (145 acres) was walled in by Henry VIII for his own pleasure and opened up by Charles II as a pleasant garden with a series of small ponds that he canalised in a decoy lake for ducks. It has remained ever since a resort of wild fowl of every variety.

Hyde Park (363¾ acres) also became Crown property and a deer forest in Henry VIII's reign. During the Civil War it was partly let out for farms and partly used for mobilising troops. In Charles II's reign it was walled in, but the public seemed to have a right of access. Queen Caroline spent £20,000 of her own money in converting the pools of the West Bourne into a lake that afterwards became known as the Serpentine.

Kensington Gardens (274½ acres) was part of the park attached to William of Orange's Palace, Kensington.

Regent's Park was formed out of Crown lands let to the Duke of Portland.

Richmond Park occupies 2358 acres. All the others except Bushy are under a thousand acres.

When the Metropolitan Board of Works was formed in 1855 the only public pleasure grounds in London were Hyde Park, Kensington Gardens, Green Park, St James's Park, Regent's Park, Primrose Hill, Greenwich Park, Victoria Park and Kennington Park.

In 1857 the Board obtained authority to lay out Finsbury Park.

There were in addition a large number of commons on the outskirts of London, survivals of the time when land was owned by village communities in common.

When individual ownership came into being the waste lands remained in the hands of the community, but under the feudal system it was held that this common land was vested in the lord of the manor subject to the rights of pasture of the free tenants. By the middle of the nineteenth century there was very little pasturing done on the London commons or of cutting turf or bracken.

They were neglected and appropriated for other purposes, mainly by railway companies, who naturally built their lines across land that was cheap, Wandsworth and Tooting Commons suffering heavily in this way.

Advancing prices in land led to the enclosure of more common land for building purposes, and nobody seemed to mind until about the middle of the century.

As late as 1851 Parliament actually approved the enclosure of Hainault Forest, and it was only by the action of the City Corporation and the Commons Preservation Society that Epping Forest was saved in 1874.

In 1866 the Metropolitan Commons Act was passed giving powers for the permanent acquisition of commons on the application of the commoners, or of any twelve ratepayers or of certain local authorities.

In this way the following commons were acquired: Blackheath, Shepherd's Bush Common, Hackney Commons, Tooting Bec Common, Clapham Common, Bostall Heath, Brook Green, Eel Brook Common, Parson's Green and Streatham Common.

These powers were later extended enabling the Board to buy and hold, in order to preserve the extinction of rights of common, any saleable rights in commons.

There were several Open Spaces Acts, which were ultimately consolidated by the Open Spaces Act in 1906.

This enabled the Council and Metropolitan Borough Councils, either separately or jointly, to buy, rent, or acquire by gift the ownership of any "open space" within or without London.

The definition of "an open space" is any land, enclosed or not enclosed, on which there are no buildings, or of which not more than one-twentieth is covered with buildings, and the whole or remainder of which is laid out as a garden or is used for purposes of recreation or lies waste.

Similar powers were granted over burial grounds closed for burial.

Some of the parks coming under the supervision of the Office of Works were not Crown property, so since 1887 Victoria, Battersea and Kennington Parks were transferred to the Metropolitan Board.

Under an Act of 1921 the Council was permitted to add dancing enclosures, and under a further Act of 1923 the Council was authorised to provide open-air swimming baths, rifle ranges, lawn-tennis courts, croquet lawns and bowling greens in addition to apparatus and equipment.

The largest open space controlled by the L.C.C. is Hainault Forest, which is over a thousand acres. Epping Forest, which is still controlled by the City of London, is 5675 acres.

The L.C.C. took over in 1889 the parks and open spaces

Kennington Park Swimming Pool (*left*), Victoria Embankment Playing Ground (*right*)

Cricket—in a Hoxton alley (*left*), and on Parliament Hill Fields (*right*)

from the Metropolitan Board of Works and in 1892 a Parks sub-department was created.

In 1933 the management of forty-one small gardens of two acres and less in various parts of the County was transferred to those Metropolitan Borough Councils in whose areas these gardens are situated.

The L.C.C. parks have grown since 1889 from 2630 acres to 6679 acres with a staff of about 1500.

People use the parks very much more than they used to, and facilities are given for enjoyment and recreation of every kind.

366 pitches for cricket, 436 pitches for football, 28 greens for bowls, three 18-hole golf courses, 29 grounds for hockey and lacrosse, 169 pitches for netball, 63 putting greens and 726 hard and grass tennis courts give you some idea of the provision made by the L.C.C. for games. There are public and private dressing rooms in the pavilions.

There are lakes and ponds for boating, with special small ponds for children's model-yacht sailing and fishing.

In nine of the L.C.C. parks there are athletic sports tracks.

Bathing has long been allowed at Highgate, Hampstead and Ken Wood and in certain other ponds, but these are being superseded by the most modern open-air swimming baths. There are now thirteen open-air swimming pools and lidos and four swimming lakes in the L.C.C. parks, one of the lidos being confined to children under twelve.

The latest lidos are at Victoria Park, Brockwell Park and Parliament Hill.

They all possess a filtration plant and there are terraces for sunbathing. Mixed bathing is now generally encouraged at practically all the swimming baths under the Council's control.

There is no question about the delight that these brightly

coloured, architecturally tasteful, spacious, airy and efficient swimming pools provide.

They certainly help more than anything else to reconcile us in hot summer days to being still in London when nearly everybody else is by the sea.

In many swimmers' eyes they are even more pleasant than the sea, for the water is always clear and blue, and the bathers can always be in the depth that best suits their taste.

In addition to the grounds provided for organised games it is nearly always possible to find dry playgrounds in the L.C.C. parks where casual games of football and cricket are encouraged.

One of the most ingenious and successful experiments carried out in recent years has been the establishment of open-air classes for school children in the parks, where organised school games and inter-school matches are also held.

There are forty-six special gymnasia fitted out for children, the equipment including sandpits and paddling pools.

The development in the variety of children's gymnasia is due to the inventive genius of the late Mr Charles Wickstead of Kettering, who always wanted the playground brought into a most conspicuous and beautiful part of the park and making it free and open to all.

When the slide, commonly known as the "Tailor's Friend", was first introduced into a park in north London slum children tramped over three miles to use it.

Mr Wickstead was also responsible for improvements in the giant stride, the see-saw on the pendulum system, the ocean wave, joy-wheel and all the other varieties of see-saw.

The children's gymnasium and dry playground at Eel

Brook Common are floodlit in the winter evenings, the gymnasium being kept open till 6.30 p.m. and the playground until 9 p.m.

Before 1922 boating in two parks, bathing, skating, model-yacht sailing and kite-flying were allowed on Sundays, and since 1922 field and court games that do not inconvenience the general public have also been allowed from 1 p.m. in winter and 2 p.m. in summer in certain parks.

Boating is allowed throughout the whole of Sunday on all the boating lakes.

In 1935 the Council allowed golf to be played throughout the day on Sundays.

Bands have always been a feature of the L.C.C. parks and open spaces during the summer.

Of recent years the performances have taken the form of band concerts of two hours' length.

In 1938 seventy bands played in forty-one parks and open spaces on Sundays and every weekday including Bank Holidays in several of these parks. In addition thirteen concert parties gave entertainments at eleven centres.

The admission charge is twopence, which includes the hire of a deck chair.

The bandstands are lit up by electricity at night and sound amplifiers are fitted.

Special entertainments for children take place on weekday afternoons in the summer holidays and prove more and more popular.

Dancing on paved areas round the bandstands was also revived in 1938.

One of the outstanding attractions of London parks is the bird and animal life to be seen there.

The varieties of wild duck, the aviaries and the deer

which are in special enclosures at Battersea Park, Golder's Hill, Victoria and Clissold Parks always arouse interest.

In Victoria and Clissold Parks there are also a few wallabies.

But most visitors go into the parks to admire the flowers and trees in which London is so rich. The woods and rock gardens, herbaceous borders and flowering trees, all help to beautify them, and in the spring and summer there are glorious displays of flowers.

Go to Ken Wood and Lesnes Abbey Wood in daffodil and bluebell time and you will forget the world outside altogether. There are rhododendrons in Dulwich Park, and fine old English gardens at Battersea, Brockwell, Golder's Hill, Kennington, Peckham Rye, Southwark, Ravenscourt, Victoria Park, and in the Rookery, Streatham Common. Here you will always get a feast of colour in summer and autumn.

There is also a sub-tropical garden at Battersea and a winter gardens and nursery at Abbey Hill.

Five parks hold chrysanthemum shows in the late autumn, admission to which is free, and attract 165,000 visitors each year.

And you may be glad to know that you can get refreshments in most of the parks.

A famous superintendent of parks described his ideal public park thus:

"An area large enough for provision to be made for most outdoor games such as football, cricket, hockey, tennis, croquet, golf and bowling, gymnasia, sandpits for the youngsters, a large lake where boating in summer and skating in winter might be enjoyed by the thousands of city dwellers who are penned up in the daytime in offices, warehouses and factories; ample space for perambulation, as well as broad well-kept lawns with fine trees and shrubs and flowers, to give that feeling of repose and refinement which to thousands is the most health-giving power city parks possess; plenty of suitable rests and shelters for the weak, the weary and aged, along with many other adjuncts which go to make for the pleasure and comfort of humanity."

That was written twenty years ago. His idea, has, I think, been amply fulfilled by the L.C.C. to-day.

Here are some outstanding features of some of the Parks.

Battersea Park (199½ acres) is the largest municipal park south of the river. Once a low-lying marsh it degenerated into a low type of fair-ground before its acquisition at a cost of about £150,000. One of its main attractions is the sub-tropical garden planted with palms. There is also an old English garden with a lily-pond and a wild garden.

Full facilities are given for all games and there are two gymnasia, a running track, and a lake of 15 acres for boating.

An enclosure has been made for deer and a sanctuary for owls.

Blackheath (267 acres) still maintains its old aspect of a heath, on which games are extensively played. The Golf Club which up till recent years used the heath as its course is the oldest in existence.

Historically Blackheath is full of interest, for it was here that London gave its welcome to Henry V after his victory at Agincourt, and to Charles II on his return from exile.

It was here that Wat Tyler collected his troops in 1381 and Jack Cade held his rendezvous in 1450.

Bostall Heath and Woods (133¼ acres). The heath, a wild and lovely place of furze, wild roses and bracken, covers a hill from which there are wide views of the Thames valley. The woods of pines, silver birch and oaks are picturesquely situated on the sides of deep gorges.

Brockwell Park (136¼ acres) is remarkable for the

retention of the garden of the old mansion of Brockwell Hall. It is surrounded with high walls, covered with roses and has a fountain in the centre with arches, old-fashioned herbs, and an old well and bucket.

This was the first garden of this kind ever to be formed in the Council's parks, and proved so popular that it was taken as a model for nearly all the others.

Clapham Common (205 acres) has no fewer than four ponds, one for model-yacht sailing, another for bathing and a third for children's boating.

Clissold Park (54½ acres), once the property of a Swedenborgian curate who married the wealthy Crawshay heiress, possesses a greater variety of animal and bird life than any other of the Council's parks. There are two aviaries, extensive deer pens, wallabies, turkeys, guinea-pigs, rabbits and fowls.

The New River flows through the park and there are two lakes, one adapted for children's boating.

Dulwich Park (72 acres) also has a lake of some three acres with boating, a small waterfall and rivulet spanned by a rustic bridge.

There is a large American garden of azaleas, rhodo-dendrons and roses.

Finsbury Park (115 acres), which cost £56,869 and an extra £50,000 to lay out, has full facilities for all games in addition to its admirable flower gardens and ornamental lake with island bird sanctuary.

Golder's Hill has a small lake planted with water-lilies and frequented by moorhens, and a second lake with tall rushes. There is also an orchard and an old English garden with pergolas, arbours, sundial, and a fountain.

Hackney Marsh (340¼ acres) provides no less than a hundred and eighty pitches for cricket and football with dressing rooms.

Hainault Forest (1108 acres), the largest open space under the control of the Council, once part of the royal and ancient forest of Waltham, was disafforested in 1851 and was replanted with gorse, broom and trees by the Council. It has a municipal golf course.

Hampstead Heath (240½ acres), which was acquired, after strenuous opposition on the part of the owners, by the Metropolitan Board of Works in 1871 for £45,000, is easily London's most popular playground, and on Bank Holidays attracts vast crowds to its swings and round-abouts. There are facilities for horse-riding, and from the rides are extensive views of London.

There is a chain of ponds at the southern end, one for bathing, and others for fishing and model-yacht sailing. There are other ponds at the Vale of Health, the White-stone pond by Jack Straw's Castle and the Leg of Mutton fringed with rushes.

Ken Wood (121 acres), which is probably the most beautiful tract of natural woodland under the Council's care, is a remnant of the ancient forest of Middlesex, and by its acquisition the preservation of the rural aspect of London's northern heights is assured for all time.

Marble Hill (66 acres) is a beautiful park running down to the river; on the left bank is Twickenham with a fine Palladian mansion, once the home of Mrs Fitzherbert.

The trees retain all their old majestic loveliness and add tremendously to the beauty of the Thames.

Parliament Hill (267¼ acres), like Hampstead Heath, has magnificent views and a chain of ponds for bathing, fishing and yachting in addition to full facilities for all games.

Plumstead Common (103 acres) provides an interesting example of the opposition that has to be overcome by the Council.

Queen's College, Oxford, the lords of the manor, having already enclosed part of Plumstead Common, enclosed the whole of Bostall Heath.

A lawsuit resulted in the defeat of the College, and the Council bought the rights of the College over the Heath.

Ruskin Park (36 acres) stands on the site of the house in which Mendelssohn wrote his "Spring Song" and near the home of John Ruskin.

Southwark Park (63 acres) has an ornamental lake with islands and overhanging trees, and sports grounds.

Springfield Park (33¾ acres) is a finely timbered ground on steep slopes overlooking the river Lea, with bandstand, tennis courts and provisions for juvenile games.

Streatham Common (66¼ acres) is one of the most picturesque pleasances in the south of London. It is an undulating gorse common with clumps of forest trees, with facilities for riding and cricket.

Tooting Common (217¾ acres) also possesses many fine trees, much gorse, a lake for fishing and children's boating, a pond for dogs and facilities for games.

Victoria Embankment Gardens (10 acres) are probably the most used in London because they are so easy to reach from the most crowded thoroughfares. They are particularly rich in music, flowers and statuary. Five days a week there are midday band performances and every evening in the season.

Victoria Park (217 acres), the largest of the L.C.C. parks, was bought in 1845 for £72,000, the proceeds of the sale of York House (now the London Museum).

This park is the playground and the garden of the East End, provision being afforded for all games. There are three lakes, including one for boating, and a large open-air swimming bath.

There are three gymnasia and a running track.

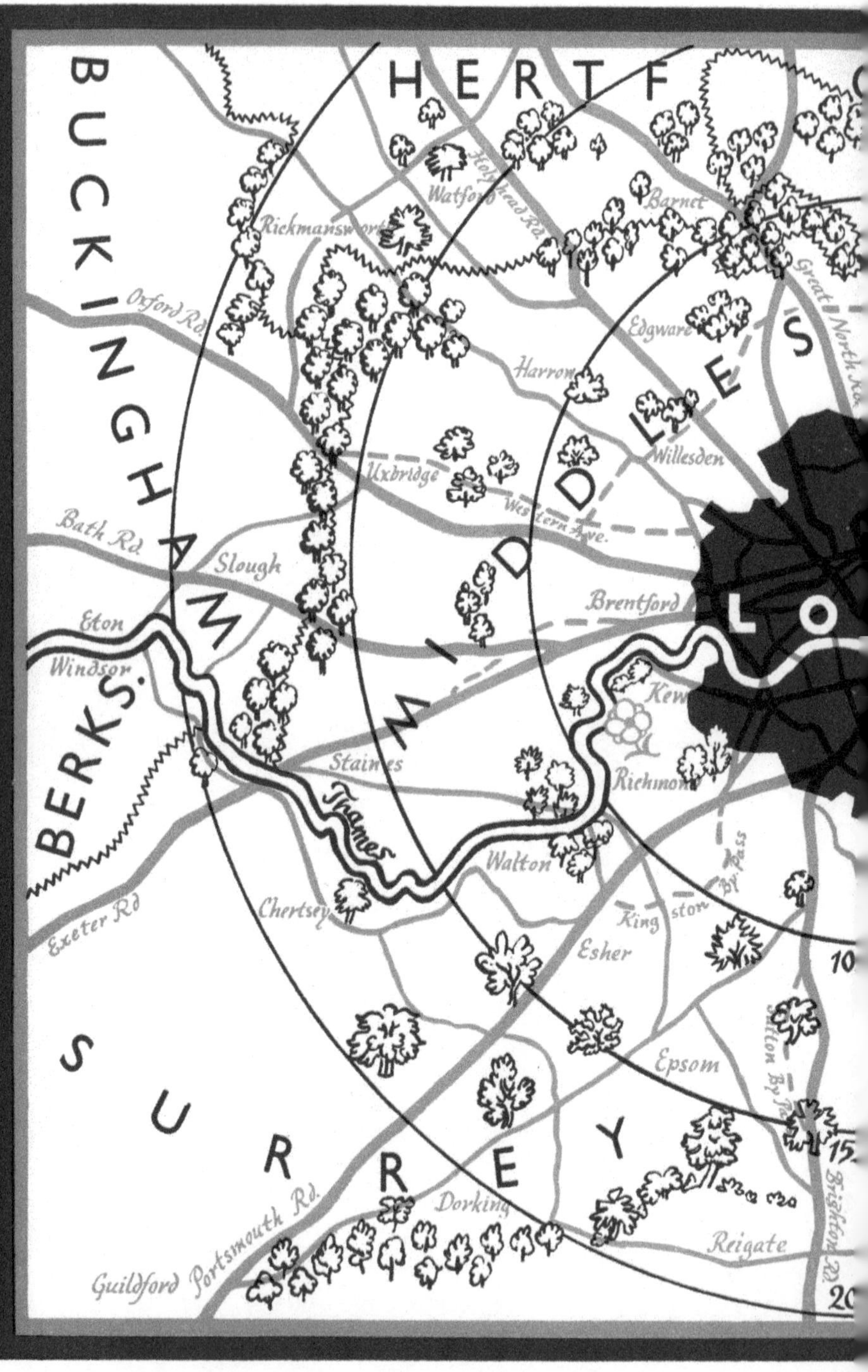

HERTF
BUCKINGHAM
MIDDLES
LO
BERKS.
SURREY
Watford
Holyhead Rd.
Barnet
Rickmansworth
Oxford Rd.
Great North Rd.
Edgware
Harrow
Willesden
Uxbridge
Western Ave.
Bath Rd.
Slough
Brentford
Eton
Windsor
Kew
Staines
Thames
Richmond
Walton
By-Pass
Chertsey
Kingston By-Pass
Exeter Rd
Esher
10
Epsom
Sutton By Pass
Brighton Rd.
Dorking
Portsmouth Rd.
Reigate
Guildford

There is an annual show of chrysanthemums.

It has, like Hyde Park, achieved fame for the number and variety of its public meetings.

Wandsworth Common (175 acres) is a good deal cut about by roads and railways but it still possesses many attractions, including a lake for fishing and facilities for all games.

Waterlow Park (26 acres) was presented to the L.C.C. by Sir Sydney Waterlow, whose statue adorns the top corner of it. His statue is the only one in London showing an umbrella.

Lauderdale House, which was visited by Pepys, stands in the grounds, which are well timbered with cedars and shrubs. There is an old English garden and a good deal of animal life.

Wormwood Scrubs (215 acres) was bought for £57,615 by the War Office and transferred to the Metropolitan Board in 1879 free of charge, on condition that the military had exclusive use of a considerable area.

The Green Belt

Land in the London area is wanted so badly for building purposes that the price of preserving green open spaces near Charing Cross not already acquired would be completely prohibitive.

So a very bold and ambitious scheme is now being tried of acquiring as much land as possible beyond the actual boundary of the County of London, but within the easy reach of Londoners by bus or tube or bicycle.

The idea of encircling the built-up area of London with a green girdle of fields and woodlands is not new.

Queen Elizabeth and James I were both anxious not to see London expand into the outlying villages. But the proclamations and laws to prevent buildings from being erected near the city had practically no effect. They were simply disobeyed.

It has been left to our own time to push forward the effort to enlarge the belt preserved from the builder for all time.

It will probably come as a surprise to you to learn that already one-tenth of the county is preserved, but the distribution is very uneven.

Westminster, Marylebone and Hackney have one-fifth of their areas occupied by open spaces, whereas Islington, Shoreditch and Southwark have less than 2 per cent.

And of course it is idle to pretend that even the largest park inside London can ever be a complete substitute for the true countryside.

The whole aim of the Green Belt is to provide within reasonable access and for ever a real countryside for the Londoner to enjoy.

Sir Christopher Wren, John Evelyn and Sir William Petty and others all wished to reconstruct London on model lines, and they had it in their power to plan a London which would have given the Londoner of to-day just the escape that he so badly needs.

But the early visionaries lacked funds, and of course as time went on and London grew the surrounding green fields were snatched up by the builders.

In 1935, however, the L.C.C. launched its magnificent scheme for bringing the Green Belt into existence.

The idea of the scheme is to secure a reserve supply of public open spaces and of recreation grounds and the establishment of a green belt or girdle of open-space lands not necessarily continuous but as near as possible to the urban areas.

The co-operation of the home counties was naturally

immediately given and the Council offered £2,000,000 to be spent over a period of three years in making grants towards the cost of securing approved lands.

The idea is not to provide an enlarged Hampstead Heath round London, but land, much of it agricultural, over which the public shall have footpath access. The important thing is that no buildings will ever be permitted on the reserved land.

The pity about this laudable scheme is that it should have come so late.

Within the memory of many middle-aged people it would have been easy to have established this belt within a radius of ten miles of Charing Cross.

But in spite of the extraordinary amount of building that has taken place since the war it is still possible to bring this Green Belt to an average distance of fifteen miles from the heart of London.

It is not of course a perfect circular belt, but roughly it stretches from Purfleet in Essex up to the L.C.C.'s great acquisition in Hainault Forest and thence to Epping Forest, one of the grandest woodlands in all England.

Then the line stretches north-west to Enfield Chase, by the Great Wood at Northaw and through extensive areas near Cockfosters and through Barnet, Watford, Rickmansworth, continuing across Harrow Weald to Harefield and Ruislip.

Thence it follows the valley of the Colne to Runnymede on the Thames, where there is fine bathing. The belt completes its circle through Eynsford, Shoreham, across Dartford Heath to the North Downs, where there are some of the finest views in the South of England.

The object in this area is to link up with the extensive properties already acquired by the National Trust along the whole ridge of the North Downs.

Up to the end of 1937 about 43,000 acres had already

been approved or provisionally approved by the Council, which has already granted or provisionally agreed to contribute £1,250,000 towards the cost.

This is equal to about 67 square miles. If it were a straight strip about a mile and a third wide it would stretch from London to Brighton.

The L.C.C. and the London Passenger Transport Board have issued a booklet on the Parks and Green Belts in which you will find descriptions of walks and rambles that you can take in the Green Belt sector, with details of how to get there by road and rail.

This will help tens of thousands of Londoners to take advantage of the joy of tramping through woodland and over the downs, looking out over the good English earth turned up by the plough, and so learn to enjoy the natural beauty that is our finest inheritance.

Chapter 7   LONDON'S BUILDINGS

It does not take long for the visitor to London to discover that it has been allowed to develop haphazard instead of being properly planned.

There are far too many private houses cheek by jowl with factories. The height of buildings bears no relation to the width of streets.

Under the Town and County Planning Act 1931 the L.C.C. becomes the town-planning authority for London.

The object is to secure an orderly redevelopment of property.

It is good estate management on a large scale and its objects are obtained by dividing areas into zones setting out the use and density prescribed.

It does not follow that any development will take place but that, if it does, it will be on the lines laid down.

A complete reorganisation of the streets and layout in

London is impossible except by buying at such a cost as to make it impracticable.

The earliest London town-planning scheme was a very small one at Streatham Common, covering only 20 acres, 5 acres of which was scheduled as public open space and the remainder for building development, with a density of ten dwelling-houses per acre.

The only scheme in operation at present is that at Highgate and Hampstead, made to preserve the amenity of the great open spaces at Hampstead Heath and Parliament Hill. In some parts not more than two houses per acre may be built.

Blocks of flats may not be erected without consent, and if the Council does consent it may lay down such conditions as it thinks fit as to height, density and proportion of site to be covered.

Proposals for a South-East District Scheme were brought forward in 1924.

An area of 7150 acres in Eltham was dealt with to secure an open space of 2000 acres. Some 450 acres of land on the wooded southern slopes of Shooter's Hill, Beckenham Place Park and Charlton Park Lake have also been preserved.

The total acreage involved in all the Council's schemes, apart from the general scheme for London, is 25,000 acres. All the schemes have the same object, to provide that as and when land comes to be developed there shall be guiding principles along the lines of which the development shall be conducted.

The L.C.C. is now engaged on formulating a scheme to cover the whole of London, with the exception of the City, and the Inner and Middle Temples and Lincoln's Inn.

London is divided into six areas for planning, the

divisions being arranged so as to group Metropolitan boroughs together.

Maps are being prepared showing zones prescribed for dwelling-houses, flats, shops, general business and industry.

Each zone will be reserved for the particular use indicated. There will also be height zones, in which buildings must not be built above a specified height without the Council's consent; and in order to secure adequate light, there will also be an angular limit.

Considerable progress has been made with a draft scheme for area IV covering the Metropolitan boroughs of Battersea and Wandsworth.

It is proposed to set aside areas as open spaces, provisions made for the preservation of trees, control of advertisements, and control of the external appearance of buildings.

Under the London Squares Preservation Act 1931 the L.C.C. has preserved, as open spaces, over 400 garden enclosures in London Squares.

The whole aim of the L.C.C. is to behave as a wise estate owner would, directing redevelopment of each part relative to the whole.

London buildings, too, are now for the first time controlled under a modern set of by-laws by which the L.C.C. has greatly increased powers over the design and protection of buildings.

By the Factories Act of 1937 means of escape has to be provided (a) in every factory in which more than twenty people are employed, (b) in every new factory employing more than ten persons above the ground floor, and (c) in every old factory employing more than ten persons above the first floor or more than 20 feet above the ground level.

This reduction from a previous limit of forty persons to ten has meant greatly increased work for the Council.

There are 9000 factories in London employing more than ten persons.

The following classes of buildings are now under the Council's control:

   (a) Buildings having any storey more than 50 feet above the ground.

   (b) Buildings containing more than twenty persons.

   (c) Buildings with shops projecting 7 feet or more.

   (d) Living rooms over any part of a building used for the storage of inflammable liquids.

   (e) Buildings having more than three storeys exceeding 30 feet in height.

Twenty-six thousand buildings have been dealt with under the means of escape provisions of the Building Acts.

The L.C.C. is the responsible authority for dangerous and neglected buildings.

Since 1869, when the duty was first carried on by the Metropolitan Board of Works, the average number of cases dealt with annually increased from 1200 to 8000.

This increase is due to the ageing of buildings, the vibration caused by traffic, and especially improved arrangements in operation for detecting dangerous cases.

For the Coronation of King George VI the L.C.C. arranged for the premises abutting over ten miles of routes to be inspected for the possible danger to spectators.

Over three hundred letters of warning were issued and the result was that there was not a single accident.

Up to 1935 the L.C.C. had renamed 2732 streets and regulated the numbers of 226,000 houses.

In 1935 the Fire Brigade and Ambulance and Post Office authorities urged that all repeated names should be abolished.

Above: Regent Street 1898
Below: Oxford Street to-day

They seemed
to get more
sun at
Charing Cross
in 1890

There still remained 3300 repetitions, about one-sixth of the total number of streets.

During 1936 and 1937 no less than 1545 streets were renamed, more than half the total number renamed during the previous forty-nine years.

The rule regarding the numbering of houses is as follows:

St Paul's Cathedral is recognised as a central point and the numbering of houses begins at the end or entrance of the street nearest to that building, except where a street leads from a main thoroughfare to a less important street, and then the numbering starts from the main thoroughfare.

Taking therefore the sides of a street as left and right (assuming that your back is towards St Paul's), the odd numbers will be on the left-hand side and the even numbers on the right-hand side.

Chapter 8   LONDON'S ROADS

Since the tramways were transferred from the control
of the L.C.C. in 1933 to the London Passenger Transport
Board the L.C.C. is no longer concerned in London traffic
except in its ferry service.

It is, however, the authority for street improvements, and
the Borough Councils, who are the highway authorities,
have to obtain the approval of the Council to do any work
of widening or improving the streets. The Council's approval is not required in the City of London.

So the L.C.C. is not a highway authority except for
most of the Thames bridges, but it has a great responsibility in dealing with the traffic problem.

Highways fall into two groups: (*a*) main routes classified
by the Ministry of Transport and (*b*) minor thoroughfares
that are unclassified.

During 1937 widening improvements have been made in Commercial Street, Finchley Road, Horseferry Road, Kensington High Street, Kilburn High Road, and York Road. It has furthermore been decided to carry out improvements at Notting Hill Gate.

A new road to connect Marylebone Road with Harrow Road was also begun in 1937.

New arterial roads to provide improved facilities for traffic passing between the new arterial roads on the outskirts of London and the central area, or proceeding across London without passing through the central areas, are either under construction or already approved.

These changes are very costly.

One of the most important is the extension of an arterial road extending from the West Cromwell Road, Kensington, to the County boundary, to be continued thereafter by the Middlesex County Council to join up with the Great Chertsey Road, the Great West Road and the North Circular Road. This will provide a valuable outlet for the traffic to the west and south-west.

Similar work has been done on the South Circular Road and the Wandsworth High Street by-pass. An additional length of the South Circular Road is now open to traffic, the road extending from Woolwich to Clapham Common.

A further type of improvement has been the construction of many "roundabouts".

The largest in South London is part of the Vauxhall Cross improvement, which included the construction of a new street passing under the Southern Railway.

No attempt at a "fly-over" bridge or vehicular subway has yet been made.

But the L.P.T.B. is gradually substituting trolley buses for trams and this too helps to make the traffic problem easier.

The L.C.C. is responsible for ten of the Thames bridges

—Albert, Battersea, Chelsea, Hammersmith, Lambeth, Putney, Vauxhall, Wandsworth, Waterloo and Westminster.

In 1937 the reconstruction of three of these, Waterloo, Chelsea and Wandsworth, was going on at the same time.

Waterloo Bridge, demolished in 1937, is superseded by a new bridge of reinforced concrete supported over piles faced with granite from the old bridge.

It will be carried over the Victoria Embankment so as to afford an uninterrupted view of the river from the Embankment.

It will accommodate six lanes of traffic, divided by refuges, and it is hoped that it will be opened in 1940.

Chelsea Bridge is a suspension bridge, with the suspension cables anchored to each end of the stiffening girders instead of to the abutments. It accommodates four lanes of traffic and was opened in May 1937.

The new Wandsworth Bridge will replace the old lattice girder bridge, which had been restricted to traffic of not more than five tons.

The steel superstructure of the new bridge will be supported by two granite-faced piers and will accommodate four lanes of traffic. The low curved lines of the bridge are designed to be in keeping with the flatness of the river bank.

The L.C.C. is also responsible for the opening bridge over Deptford Creek and for about fifty other County bridges over streams, rivers and canals, including Barking Road Bridge, Highgate Archway and Bow Bridge.

A new opening bridge at Glamis Road was completed in August 1937. It is a rolling lift bridge electrically operated and replaces a very narrow swing bridge.

The L.C.C. is also responsible for the tunnels under the

Waterloo Bridge—as it will be

Waterloo Bridge—as it was

Above: Thames Tunnel
Below: Woolwich Ferry

lower reaches of the Thames, where the existence of low-level bridges would interfere with shipping.

The pedestrian tunnels at Greenwich and Woolwich have a 9 foot footway and are 1217 and 1655 feet long respectively.

The vehicular tunnels at Rotherhithe and Blackwall are 16 feet wide and 6278 and 6118 feet long respectively.

There is going to be a duplicate tunnel at Blackwall to relieve the cross-river traffic.

Woolwich ferry, opened in 1889, is the only free public service ferry in England.

Nearly 4000 vehicles and over 7000 pedestrians cross it every day.

The service is maintained by four boats of a special paddle-wheel type, and each boat carries 1000 passengers and a total weight of 100 tons.

The L.C.C. is no longer responsible for the roads running alongside the Thames, but its $6\frac{3}{4}$ miles of river embankment walls act as the flood defence for these highways.

The L.C.C. maintains nine miles of pipe subways. These twenty-four subways accommodate the pipes and mains and cables of the utility companies and all repairs are carried out in the subway.

The L.C.C. also owns a pier at Greenwich, a very popular promenade, from which 200,000 visitors watch the passing river traffic in the course of a year.

Pleasure steamers to the south and east coasts call at the pier in the summer to pick up passengers, and launches to Westminster leave at regular and frequent intervals. About 250,000 passengers land or embark during the season.

Chapter 9   LONDON'S POOR

The L.C.C. exists to protect the citizens of London.

In the department of Public Assistance its duty is to ensure that no Londoner shall suffer the worst extremes of poverty.

No fewer than 4300 members of the L.C.C. staff are occupied solely in this business of relieving the distress of those who are hardest hit and unable to fend for themselves.

The guiding principle in their work is to provide as far as possible individual help for those who through poverty are unable to secure it for themselves.

The annual cost of providing this help comes to over £3,000,000.

The Public Assistance service has its origin in a Poor Law Statute of 1601, by which each parish was called upon to make provision for

"Settinge to worke all such persons maried or unmaried

having no means to maintaine them, use no ordinarie and dailie trade of lief to get their livinge by...."

And for relieving "the lame impotente olde blinde and suche other amonge them beinge poore and not able to work".

The duties were carried out by "overseers" who, with the churchwardens, had the thankless job of raising funds by taxing every inhabitant in their parish.

In 1834, by the Poor Law Amendment Act, the "overseers" were superseded by boards of "guardians of the poor" elected by the ratepayers. The Commissioners appointed under this Act aimed at discouraging outdoor relief and made public assistance conditional on entry into the workhouse, which became the real test of destitution. It also provided for the union of Parishes. London had thirty separate Boards of Guardians for nearly a hundred years.

From 1 April 1930 the L.C.C., as the result of the Local Government Act 1929, became the sole authority for the provision of public assistance in London, the county being divided into ten areas. It had suddenly to assume responsibility for 140 hospitals, schools and other institutions, providing 75,000 beds, 180,000 people in receipt of relief and expenditure of £11,000,000 a year.

The principal business of the Public Assistance Committee is to provide requisite help for poor people.

This is done mainly by granting weekly allowances of "outdoor relief" or by care and maintenance in institutions and elsewhere.

It helps people who are temporarily ill and unable to exist on their National Health Insurance benefit, and those who find it impossible to live on their pensions.

Training is given in occupational trades and handicrafts.

In each of the ten areas is a local office, and each area is divided into relief districts, of which there are some two hundred.

A relieving officer is appointed for each relief district, and there are seventy relief stations at which applications for relief can be made.

As soon as he gets an application for relief the relieving officer makes enquiries and visits the applicant's home.

If the need is urgent he has the power to meet it at once, e.g. by giving food tickets, issuing orders for admission to institutions, or arranging for attendance by the district medical officer. He has no power however to issue money.

He reports these applications to an adjudicating officer. Up till 1935 these reports had to go before a sub-committee, but except for certain specified types of cases the adjudicating officer, after interviewing the applicant, can now decide whether relief is necessary and if so the nature and amount of assistance to be given.

The general standard of amounts, apart from rent allowance, is for one adult living with relatives 9s. a week, for an adult not living with relatives 10s., for two adults living together 18s., for two adults and one child 22s. with 3s. for each additional child. Allowances are added for coal and extra nourishment.

The average weekly number of persons receiving outdoor relief in London in 1937 was 79,000, and the average weekly cost was £32,300.

The total amount spent on outdoor relief during 1937 was £1,700,000.

In December of that year an increase of 1s. a week was made for old people, old couples living alone, and in respect of children of ten and over, and this cost about £80,000 a year.

Non-residential training centres were established to give

able-bodied men in receipt of outdoor relief a training in carpentry, woodwork, boot-repairing, sign-writing or some other useful occupation.

This training is required by a statutory order, but the men work with a will and have achieved a remarkable degree of skill in handicraft after very little tuition. They are required to attend for 20 hours a week and tea is provided in the afternoon.

At the training centre at Old Montague Street, Whitechapel, I saw a showroom of some of the men's achievements which ran from models of old sailing ships to iron and steel toolmaking, and all the men who were at work on boot repairs or clothes pressing for the institutions agreed that it was a great deal better than loitering about the streets with nothing to do.

There are, of course, cases where outdoor relief is unsuitable.

For these the L.C.C. has provided residential establishments accommodating 11,000 inmates.

There are thirteen institutions in London containing some 9000 inmates.

When they were taken over from the Board of Guardians most of them contained every type of inmate, old and young, able-bodied and infirm, sick and mental cases and children.

The L.C.C. is reorganising these institutions so that each shall be reserved for the type of inmate most suitable.

This means the scrapping of unsatisfactory buildings and the adaptation of others, and I had the good fortune to see the actual change-over in the Marylebone Institution.

Old men and old women were supplied with comfortable quarters equipped with tiled bathrooms, excellently lit and well-ventilated day rooms and dormitories, electric lifts, and serving hatches from the servery to the dining rooms ensuring hot plates and expeditious service.

The men were supplied with billiard tables, dart boards and skittle alleys, while the women knitted in rooms lavishly decorated with flowers and pictures.

I was particularly struck by the variety of colour and design in the women's dresses, shawls and cardigans.

Radio sets are fitted into most of the day-rooms and there are comfortable arm-chairs in which to lie back and listen.

There is a good library where books can be changed every other day, and there is both an Established church and a Catholic chapel.

Nonconformists use the Church of England chapel.

The walls of all rooms are painted in bright tones of yellow and green, and the floors are of red jarrow wood.

The grounds are being converted into walks and gardens.

I inspected the admirable central kitchen and watched the old men come in to their midday meal in the great hall.

The tables were covered with blue check tablecloths.

I saw heaped-up plates of boiled bacon and beans being handed down the tables, each man's ration (a very generous one) being exactly weighed as it was transferred to his plate.

The older men and women are free to come and go pretty well as they like, returning to the institution only for their meals if they feel so inclined, but the majority seem to prefer the society of others and stay in their own little groups.

Londoners in particular like society, and they certainly like to watch the traffic of the Marylebone Road.

A very great change has come over this institution since the days when it contained padded cells and maternity wards, and the mentally deranged were under the same roof as the young children.

To-day the whole object of the L.C.C. is to separate types as far as possible, and now in the Marylebone Institution you will only find three classifications, the able-bodied who are capable of continuous work, the healthy old who can potter about, and the infirm who are incapable of getting to and from the dining hall, but can get from their day-rooms to their dormitories, which are now on the same floor. Drinking-water is supplied on every floor.

There are married quarters for husbands and wives who wish to live together, but they are not popular.

If, as I was told, a couple have been happily married for many years they will do everything in their power to preserve their independence outside an institution. If they have been unhappy together they will welcome the chance of getting away from each other.

Yet the married quarters are very cosy and comfortable, with a little communal dining room and neat little private bedrooms where they can keep their treasures.

Voluntary workers from the Brabazon Society come to the institutions at frequent intervals to give tuition in rug-making, basket-weaving and fancy work for sales of work to provide extra comforts for the inmates.

In addition to these twelve institutions there are three homes for the aged, at one of which, Cedars Lodge, great headway has been made with vegetable and flower gardens cultivated by the old men.

The aim of the L.C.C. now is to remove whenever possible the lack of privacy which threatens sometimes to destroy the harmony of those inmates who wish to be quiet and by themselves.

Two residential centres at Sutton, Surrey, and Dunton,

4·2

Essex, cater for the needs of able-bodied unemployed men. At Sutton men are taught the trades of bricklaying, plastering, hairdressing, and motor repair work, while at Dunton Farm men are taught carpentering and farming.

About 800 men pass through these two centres in a year and most of them are discharged to employment.

There are two Children's Receiving Homes at Fulham and Wandsworth where children between the ages of three and sixteen are accommodated usually for about a fortnight before being transferred to residential schools or homes.

Voluntary organisations also accommodate special cases of cripples, deaf and dumb, incurables, backward and difficult boys and girls and unmarried mothers, and use is made of some eighty of these establishments by the L.C.C.

In the nine casual wards you may find on any night as many as 700 men.

Finally, in the L.C.C. Hostel at Mount Pleasant there is accommodation for seventy-six men, where they can stay while efforts are made to get them back into employment.

There remains the problem of London's homeless.

Our first instinct when an obviously homeless man asks one for the price of a night's lodging is to give it to him quickly and without question.

We give the money quickly as a sort of sop to our own consciences. We no longer feel quite so ashamed of going back to our own firesides, good meals and warm beds once we have planted a copper or two into these pleaders' hands. They, of course, are banking on that.

But it is with some surprise that we learn from the L.C.C. that in doing this we are probably doing more harm than good.

Our duty, if we really care for the welfare of the man, and not just our own private feelings, is to tell him to go to the L.C.C. Welfare Office under Charing Cross Railway bridge at the Embankment end of Northumberland Avenue.

No man or woman in London need be homeless. There are beds and to spare for all comers. So if people sleep out they sleep out because they like it.

If then we give money for this purpose it is unlikely to be spent on a bed.

We may feel, as Doctor Johnson and Charles Lamb felt, that to subsist on indiscriminate charity keeps a man free, and certainly no one wishes to increase the number of men who habitually use the casual wards.

But the man who is content to go on trading on our charitable instincts to keep himself alive has sunk about as low as a man can sink, and the L.C.C. has undertaken the difficult business of trying to rehabilitate every man who comes for help.

Indeed it has for centuries been a tradition in London that men and women should never lack roof or bed.

It is by no means the cold-hearted city that it has been made out to be.

Ever since Queen Elizabeth's reign there have been laws about the relief of destitution in this form.

Every evicted tenant of a London house has a right, by law, to admittance to an institution. Any wanderer has a right to a bed in a casual ward.

Indeed, as you doubtless know, sleeping out is a legal offence.

And yet as recently as just before the war, in 1912, you would find over a thousand homeless people in the London streets every night.

To counteract what was known as the "scandal of the Embankment" the Metropolitan Asylums Board (a body representing the various London Boards of Guardians) established its Homeless Poor Night Office on the Victoria Embankment, to which the police could direct any homeless person with a ticket, which was there exchanged for a card of admission to one of the homes there recommended.

This had the excellent result of reducing the number of sleepers-out by one-half in less than a year, and in 1934 it had been reduced to about eighty nightly.

People still continued, however, to use "sit-up" shelters in church crypts, chapels and other places, where they got no chance of undressing and washing and sanitary accommodation was nearly always inadequate.

A further objection to these "sit-up" shelters is that they encourage the same sort of drifting that indiscriminate giving does. No steps are taken to give each man a chance to get back his self-respect by getting regular employment.

The Night Office was only open from 10 p.m. to 2 a.m. The Public Assistance Committee of the L.C.C. therefore in 1935 turned the Night Office into the present "Welfare Office", which is open all the year round from 10 a.m. till 2 a.m. the next morning.

Any homeless man or woman can walk through the open door to the waiting room until the interviewing officer is free to enquire into the special needs of that case.

This office is purely a clearing house and distributes its callers to the appropriate agency by providing a letter of introduction, a ticket or voucher for the bus or tram journey and instructions how to reach the hostel.

There are thirty of these hostels in close touch with the Welfare Office.

During the year ending 31 March 1937, 14,000 men and 300 women were helped through the Welfare Office. About three-quarters of the applicants come from the provinces, and about half of them are young men under thirty. Over 85 per cent of the applicants are sent to the homes and hostels of voluntary societies.

A careful register is kept of all cases and this had reached by September 1937 a total of 37,500.

The applicant may be provided with food and lodging until he can fend for himself. He may stay for recuperation for several weeks. He may undergo a course of occupational training at the Sutton Training Centre.

Among the voluntary societies which co-operate with the L.C.C. in this scheme are the British Legion, the C.O.S., the Church Army, the Council of Social Service, the Salvation Army, St Martin-in-the-Fields, the S.O.S. Society, Toc H, the 'Morning Post' Embankment Home, the Fellowship of St Christopher, and the Embankment Fellowship Centre.

The L.C.C. has its own hostel at Mount Pleasant, where men are maintained while efforts are made to put them back into employment.

There are also nine casual wards in the Metropolitan area where a man is given a hot bath, a bed in a heated cubicle or dormitory, a clean night shirt and facilities for washing and mending his clothes.

In all London, however, it was found as far back as 1930 that thirty-nine beds were all that were necessary for women casuals.

Captain Hotchin, the superintendent of the Welfare Office, told me that very few of those who come to him are habitual vagrants.

The newer type of wanderer is a lorry-jumper or "hitch-hiker", who relies on car-owners to bring him along the road.

A considerable underhand trade is done in the return halves of excursion tickets which leaves many men destitute in London.

Some come up to London on the proceeds of their insurance benefit, some because they have domestic or criminal reasons for escaping from home.

Sometimes a man loses heart over his lost job, at others a man quarrels with his wife. Sometimes a whole family will find itself stranded. Occasionally a boy arrives who has run away from school. Often an ex-convict will appear.

There is a special hostel for women at Carisbrooke House, but the problem of women is much less urgent than that of men.

Sometimes a young girl will appear who has "jumped a lorry" and wished that she hadn't, occasionally a wife of a man once rich who has gone to gaol and left her penniless, and I heard of a couple of elderly sisters who quarrelled violently but could not bear to be separated.

They were the daughters of an Army Officer left destitute. One had been married, the other was a spinster. They tried to live by doing jobs of cleaning. Then they were reduced to sleeping out, with a night or two in the poorest lodging-houses when they could afford it.

The L.C.C. Welfare Officer sent them to the Salvation Army, which provided them with a room and furniture and the L.C.C. placed them on outdoor relief.

These are a few instances of the way in which the L.C.C. ensures, so far as is humanly possible, that none of its citizens shall be destitute or live without a roof over their heads.

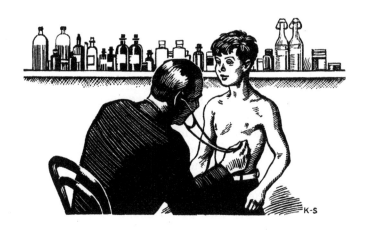

Health Services

The first Act of Parliament dealing with Public Health was passed in 1388, wherein it was ordained that all filth and garbage should be at once removed from the ditches and rivers, where it corrupted and infected the air and caused intolerable diseases.

Kennels to carry off sewage and rain water had been in use for a century before that, and every householder was responsible for clearing away all dirt from his door, and discouraged from throwing refuse and water out of his windows.

Rakyers or rakers were hired to cleanse the streets, and in Edward III's reign twelve carts were kept at the City's expense to clear away the refuse and sewage. About one-fifth of London's population died of plague in the early seventeenth century and plague was so rampant when

James I came to the throne that Parliament could not be summoned till nine months after the Coronation.

As late as 1628 we hear of complaints of filth lying in the streets. There were of course no sewers and plague was in consequence likely to break out at any time.

It was the Great Fire of 1666 that proved to be London's turning-point in sanitation. The fire swept away the accumulated filth of centuries and the Act for rebuilding the City of London passed in 1667 really was the origin of the Commissioners of Sewers for the City of London, who were the real fathers of the London County Council.

For two hundred years this body looked after the sanitary well-being of the City.

Outside the City each parish managed its own affairs, appointing its own surveyors and scavengers.

Michael Angelo Taylor's Act of 1817 systematised the provisions relating to paving and improvement of streets and cleansing of drains.

The invention of the water-closet came a few years before this, but this discharged not into the sewers but into a cesspool. Overflow drains had then to be introduced to connect the cesspools with the street sewers.

At first it was an offence to discharge offensive matter in the sewers. Within a few years (by 1847) it had become compulsory to do so. These sewers were originally banked-up open water courses.

In 1847 the sewerage of the districts now forming the County of London was governed by seven commissions. With so many different agencies it was impossible to get any general principle of drainage.

In 1843 the Poor Law Commissioners drew attention to the defective state of the sewerage and drainage of the London district and to the inadequacy of the existing law.

This led to the Metropolitan Commission of Sewers, which abolished in a few years about 200,000 cesspools and compulsorily substituted water-closets, draining them into the sewers.

In consequence the Thames soon became little more than an open sewer, the banks between Westminster and Waterloo Bridges becoming covered with vast accumulations of foul and offensive mud at low tide. Six more commissions were appointed between 1848 and 1855.

At last in 1855 the Metropolitan Board of Works was created, whose primary duty was to maintain the main sewers and construct new ones. It is important to notice that it was at this stage that all duties relating to paving, lighting, watering and cleansing of streets were delegated to local authorities, as they still are.

The Sanitary Act of 1866 marked another great step in the development of sanitary law; henceforth "overcrowding" was declared to be a nuisance, and dangerous infectious diseases were at last dealt with.

The Local Government Act of 1888 made the L.C.C. the central authority for health in London.

The Public Health Act 1891 codified and simplified all the complexities of the law in respect of this service.

The Board now constructed three main intercepting sewers on each side of the river, converging on the north side at Abbey Mills, West Ham and on the south side at Deptford Creek, and thence continuing to Barking and Crossness respectively, where the contents were discharged into the river.

All the old sewers were more or less reconstructed, some of them being offensive open sewers, and storm-water sewers were constructed to take and carry away the water produced by exceptionally heavy falls of rain.

The natural result of these measures was a cleaning up

of the river in London but a pollution in the neighbour-
hood of the outfalls.

As a result of a Royal Commission it was decided that
the solid matter should be separated and disposed of, and
works were erected for the precipitation and chemical
clarification of the sewage. The solids, known as sludge,
were carried by five steam sludge ships far out to sea.

Further sewers were added in 1901; low-level sewer
no. 2, Hammersmith to Bow; middle-level sewer no. 2,
Willesden to Old Ford; Hackney to Abbey Mills; Isle of
Dogs; north outfall sewer and Abbey Mills pumping
station enlargement.

On the south side were added southern high-level sewer,
Nunhead to Crossness; southern low-level sewer no. 2,
Battersea to Deptford; southern outfall sewer, Deptford to
Crossness; southern outfall enlargement and Deptford
pumping station enlargement.

Storm-relief sewers were also added.

To-day the Abbey Mills is capable of lifting 1000 tons
40 feet a minute; the steamers carry 1500 tons of sludge
57 miles out to sea.

A gas for lighting purposes much richer than coal gas
is made out of the digested sludge at Beckton.

There are now about 400 miles of main, intercepting
and storm-relief sewers, five main stations for pumping
the dry-weather flow and storm water and seven stations
for pumping storm water only.

The total cost of the sewers and pumping stations since
1855 has been nearly £17,000,000. The rate works out at
4d. in the £.

The cleansing and scavenging of the streets, the removal
of house and trade refuse, the maintenance of local sewers,
and the provision and maintenance of public conveniences
are duties of the City of London Corporation and the
Metropolitan Borough Councils.

The L.C.C. is responsible for the cleansing and scavenging of the Thames tunnels and bridges other than those in the City, and for the provision of public conveniences in its parks.

Before the Local Government Act 1929 the bodies concerned with public health in London included the Ministry of Health (up to 1919 the Local Government Board), the L.C.C. (established 1889), the Metropolitan Borough Councils (established 1899), the Corporation of the City of London (from medieval times), the London Port Sanitary Authority (established 1872), the Metropolitan Water Board (established 1903), the London Insurance Committee (established 1912), the Metropolitan Asylums Board (established 1867), Boards of Guardians (established 1834), the Ministry of Pensions and the Home Office, whose Factory department supervises the hygiene of factories and workshops and occupational diseases.

This multiplicity of offices has now been reduced.

The Ministry of Health is responsible for the supervision of medical, maternity, sickness and disablement benefits, the first being administered through the insurance committees, the others through Approved Societies.

The twenty-eight Metropolitan boroughs are responsible for administering the acts relating to drainage, for suppressing nuisances, including those caused by smoke and noise, supervising offensive trades, cowsheds, slaughter-houses, common and seamen's lodging-houses, repairing houses and closing single unfit houses and small clearance areas, looking after burial grounds and crematoria, destroying rats and mice, disinfecting houses and persons, looking after the sanitation and conditions of shops (the L.C.C., however, controls the hours and the half-day closing), collecting and disposing of household refuse, controlling food supply (including milk) and looking after baths and wash-houses.

They are also responsible for the control of infectious and epidemic diseases (the L.C.C. provides the fever hospitals), vaccination, tuberculosis dispensaries, maternity and child welfare, notification of births, foster children, registration of births and deaths, first-aid posts, decontamination and supply of gas masks for air raids.

The City of London has all the functions of the Metropolitan Borough Councils and many of those administered by the County Council.

The County Council is the Hospital, Public Assistance and Education Authority for the City, but the City provides its own ambulance service, venereal disease clinic, tuberculosis dispensary and mental hospital. It is worth remembering that the resident population of the City is under 10,000.

The London Port Health Authority exercises its authority up to Teddington Lock, and its duties include the examination of passengers and crews of in-bound vessels from foreign ports, inspection of imported food, inspection of ships and boats and the prevention of nuisances. It also provides for the medical inspection of aliens arriving by sea.

The Metropolitan Water Board is solely concerned with the supply of water within the London area.

The London Insurance Committee administers medical benefit for the insured.

The Metropolitan Asylums Board, which was abolished in 1930, had to provide hospitals for fever, tuberculosis, children, certain mental cases and a training ship for boys. It also administered the casual wards.

Until April 1930 there were twenty-five Boards of Guardians who provided hospitals and institutions for the destitute, ranging from general hospitals admitting a large number of acute medical and surgical cases to old workhouses admitting a wide range of the sick and destitute: they were responsible for outdoor relief and outdoor medical relief. They were also responsible for the registration of births and deaths and vaccination. All these functions except the last group, which now belongs to the Metropolitan Borough Councils, were transferred to the L.C.C. on the disappearance of the Guardians.

The Ministry of Pensions provides hospitals for disabled pensioners of the Great War.

The Home Office concerns itself with occupational diseases, safety and conditions in factories and workshops. The inspection of these workshops is undertaken by the Boroughs, that of the factories by factory inspectors working under the Home Office.

This still leaves the L.C.C. with the major responsibilities. These include main drainage, large-scale housing, making by-laws with regard to sanitation, promotion of Parliamentary Bills, examination for tuberculosis of milk, inspection of cows until 1938, when this work was taken over by the Ministry of Agriculture, provision for large open spaces and swimming baths and town planning.

So far as personal health services are concerned the L.C.C. is responsible for the tuberculosis scheme, venereal diseases, school medical services, supervision of midwives, certain maternity and child-welfare services administered voluntarily, registration of nursing homes, welfare of the blind, mental deficiency and lunacy Acts, accident ambulance service, general ambulance service, control of infectious diseases among school children, hospitals, including general, fever, tuberculosis, and children's; the district medical service under Poor Law Acts, complete administration of the casual wards, Poor Law institutions, children's receiving homes and residential children's homes (these are administered under the Public Assistance or Education

Departments), grants for district nursing and duties in connection with hospitals and ambulances in time of war.

The history of the development of the general hospitals can be traced back to the Middle Ages, when hospitals were guest-houses in which the demands of hospitality often included ministrations to a sick wayfarer.

The Church undertook the relief of destitution and the care of the sick poor until the dissolution of the monasteries, when great hardship was experienced by those who had been taken care of by the Church.

In the Poor Law Act of 1601 the overseers of the poor were empowered to collect sums for and towards the necessary relief of the lame, impotent, old, blind and unemployed, the idle who wouldn't work and the impotent who couldn't work. The poorhouse from the sixteenth to the eighteenth century was a cottage or group of cottages used as free lodgings for parish pensioners, a receptacle for disabled and sick and temporary shelter for tramps.

In 1722 power was conferred on parishes to provide houses and maintain the poor.

In 1782 Gilbert's Act gave power for poorhouses to which only the old, sick and infirm were to be sent.

From the parish poorhouse came the parish workhouse. Right down to 1834 there was intermixing of healthy and sick, sane and insane, all undergoing the same treatment and supplied with precisely the same kind of attention, or lack of it, care and food.

The Reform Act of 1832 led to reform of the Poor Law. In 1847 came the Poor Law Board, which was dissolved in 1871.

By the Metropolitan Poor Act 1867 provision was made for the establishment of dispensaries and asylums for sick, insane and infirm, and it was not until this that provision was made for separate treatment of the sick by the esta-

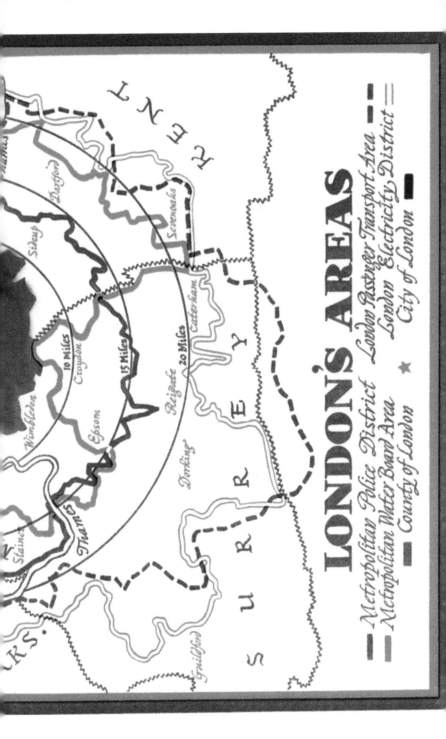

LONDON'S AREAS

Metropolitan Police District London Passenger Transport Area
Metropolitan Water Board Area London Electricity District
County of London ★ City of London

KENT

Dartford

Sidcup

Sevenoaks

Caterham

10 Miles
Croydon

15 Miles

20 Miles

Reigate

Epsom

Wimbledon

Dorking

Thames

Staines

SURREY

Guildford

...KS.

blishment of workhouse infirmaries. This Act also provided for the employment of paid and qualified nurses, and that all medicines should be supplied at the charge of the guardians and not out of the salaries of the medical officers.

The earliest infirmaries were St Pancras 1868, St George and the Earl Wandsworth and St Mary Abbotts 1871, Shoreditch 1872, Chelsea 1873, and Hackney 1874. The first to establish a training school for nurses was St Marylebone in 1884.

The workhouses were now transformed into general hospitals with new airy wards with a resident doctor, trained nurses and a scientific dietary.

General voluntary hospitals scarcely existed anywhere except in London down to the beginning of the eighteenth century. A few London hospitals survived from the Middle Ages. St Bartholomew's (1123) and St Thomas' (1200) managed to survive, and these were supplemented in the eighteenth century by Westminster (1719), Guy's (1725), St George's (1733), London (1740) and Middlesex (1745). In the nineteenth century followed Charing Cross (1818), Seamen's (1821), Royal Free (1828), University College (1833), King's (1839), St Mary's (1851) and Royal Northern (1856).

The transfer to the L.C.C. in 1930 of the duties of the Boards of Guardians and of the Metropolitan Asylums Board naturally meant an enormous expansion of the public health work devolving upon it. It meant taking over of seventy-six hospitals and institutions containing over 42,000 beds and a staff of 20,000 persons. There are 112 voluntary hospitals with 15,304 beds. Some 30 per cent of the patients receiving treatment in the London voluntary hospitals reside outside the County boundary.

The birth-rate has gone down from 30 per thousand between 1891 and 1900 to 13·6 in 1936, the death-rate has also gone down from 19·2 to 12·5. Marriages have gone up from 17·8 to 21·1. Infant mortality has been reduced from 159 to 66.

There is a satisfactory lowering of the death-rate from tuberculosis and other once common diseases.

The health of the people has been preserved by improved systems of drainage, proper removal of household refuse, the establishment of a pure water supply and the provision of good houses to take the place of the old germ-breeding slums.

An immense improvement has resulted from the work of the school medical service.

During the first half of the period since education has become compulsory, no attention whatever was paid to the physical condition of the children, but during the second half doctors, dentists and nurses have all been roped in to form the very important school medical service.

In 1899 the Elementary Education (Defective and Epileptic Children) Act authorised the establishment of special schools for mentally and physically defective children, as the result of which it became necessary to examine and certify the children.

Before this, however, Mr Brudenell Carter, the famous eye surgeon, was permitted to survey the elementary schools and reported a mass of children with defective vision intensified by the absence of correction by appropriate spectacles.

In 1900 the School Board appointed six part-time oculists to test the children's vision.

The loss of grant owing to the absence of children in great numbers through parasitic disease led to the appointment of the first school nurse.

It was computed that 20,000 children were at any given moment suffering from ring worm.

During the whole of 1937 only 181 fresh cases were reported.

A Medical Department was formed in 1902 under Dr James Kerr, but there was no power to provide treatment. Starving children could not be fed by the education society and the voluntary hospitals could not cope with the flood of children.

Royal Commissions were set up and in 1906 the Education (Provision of Meals) Act at last gave the education authorities power to feed the starving children.

The Administrative Provisions Act of 1907 made periodical medical inspection of school children compulsory.

In the same year the Council tackled the problem of verminous children, and such large numbers of children attended the out-patients' departments of hospitals that one eye surgeon had to fight his way through them.

School treatment centres and clinics had therefore to be opened—the first was at Kilburn in 1911—and to-day there are ninety-five centres dealing with eye, ear and teeth troubles.

Each local authority was compelled to appoint a school medical officer.

By 1912 the Medical Officer of Health also became the school medical officer, the first holder of the dual offices being Sir William Hamer.

The first dental treatment centres were opened in 1911 in Deptford and Southwark, and the dentists engaged visited the nearby schools and inspected the children there. Dental inspections in all schools every year is now the rule.

While healthy children are possibly not seen more than four times a year, ailing and defective children are kept under constant observation. Over 400 school nurses are now employed in the London School Medical Service.

Their main duty is to see that the children are clean and remove any chance of danger of contagion spreading through the schools. Every child is seen at least once a term by the school nurse and is weighed and measured every six months.

There are also 5000 voluntary workers helping in the physical care service. The teachers give lessons in hygiene and do their best to promote enjoyment in physical exercises.

Children with any tendency to tuberculosis are sent, if need be, to open-air day or residential sanatoria.

Twenty supervisory centres and 800 beds in county hospital schools for children suffering from rheumatism have been established. Open-air education is provided in fifteen day and seven residential schools and in 230 open-air classes attached to day schools, and this helps to cure many cases of those predisposed to tuberculosis.

By the Local Government Act of 1929 the hospital and convalescent beds of the authority can now be used for the needy schoolchild, and in 1936, 4500 children received convalescence in the Council's institutions.

Another scheme which has made great strides is the Tuberculosis Scheme. Before 1930 the L.C.C. did not own any institutions for the treatment of tuberculosis, but by the Local Government Act of 1929 the institutions transferred from the Metropolitan Asylums Board included eleven institutions with 2300 beds approved for the treatment of this disease.

In 1934 they were presented by the United Services Fund with the Heatherwood Hospital, Ascot, with its 136 beds for children suffering from surgical tuberculosis. It has now been enlarged by 100 beds.

The Poor Law Institutions had of course their complement of tuberculosis cases, but since 1933 the L.C.C. has arranged that all residential treatment for tuberculosis should come under its special tuberculosis scheme.

The beds provided in the L.C.C. tuberculosis institutions by 1934 amounted to 2377, including 954 for children. In the general hospitals 1130 beds were occupied by tuberculosis patients and almost the same number at voluntary institutions.

Two units, one of 100 beds at the Brompton Hospital and one of 50 at St George's Home, Chelsea, were kept for observation purposes, where the medical staff have a chance of observing the patients' response to treatment.

Pulmonary tuberculosis in children is particularly difficult to diagnose, and so doubtful cases are subjected to intensive observation at the High Wood Hospital, Brentwood.

The L.C.C. makes arrangements for the boarding-out of children living in heavily infected homes, and has instituted six open-air day schools for pulmonary, glandular and abdominal cases with 475 pupils.

Among the institutions to which patients are sent are the Cambridgeshire Tuberculosis Colony at Papworth, the Preston Hall Colony at Aylesford, Kent, and the Burrow Hill Colony at Frimley where long-period treatment is combined with training in gardening or clerical work.

The aim of tuberculosis schemes is to relieve the needs of individual sufferers, and to provide ways of reducing the occurrence of the disease.

The deaths from pulmonary tuberculosis in London have sunk from 1382 per million in 1911 to 705 in 1937, and from non-pulmonary tuberculosis from 389 to 86.

The L.C.C. has provided sanatoria for adults at King George V Sanatorium, Godalming, Pinewood Sanatorium, Wokingham, St Luke's Hospital, Lowestoft, Grove Park

Hospital, S.E., Colindale Hospital, Hendon, Northern
Hospital, Winchmore Hill, and St George's Home,
Milman's Street, Chelsea.

There are sanatoria for children at High Wood, Brentwood, Queen Mary's Hospital, Carshalton, Millfield,
Rustington, as well as at Heatherwood, Ascot, which I
mentioned before.

The total number of patients admitted to residential
treatment in 1937 under the tuberculosis scheme was
8977, the total number discharged during the year was
6807 and the number died was 1895.

The L.C.C. directs the largest hospital service in the
world. Any resident in the County of London is at liberty
to take advantage of these hospitals, which are divided
into two divisions, general and special.

The general hospitals provide for the treatment of all
kinds of acute and chronic illness, except infectious disease.
There are forty-five of these hospitals with a total bed
accommodation of 23,197. These hospitals include twenty-
eight acute hospitals, twelve hospitals for chronic sick
patients (including an institution for infirm patients), two
convalescent hospitals and two hospitals for sane epileptics.

Of these forty-five general hospitals forty-four were
formerly Poor Law Institutions which have been appropriated by the Council.

The Council has appropriated as general hospitals
certain Poor Law Institutions. Since 1930, 20,822 beds
have been transferred in this way.

To meet the increasing demand for beds a new general
hospital for acute patients is to be erected on a site adjacent
to St Benedict's Hospital, Church Lane, Tooting. This
will be the first general hospital built by the Council and
will incorporate all the latest developments in hospital
planning and equipment.

In 1937 a mental observation block of seventy-six beds was erected at St Pancras Institution. This was the first psychiatric unit planned and built for its specific purpose.

St Francis' Hospital, formerly known as Constance Road Institution, has been converted into a hospital for cases of chronic sickness and of mental disorder.

A nurses' home of 265 bedrooms has been completed at Hackney and is the largest home erected by the Council.

The special hospitals include the fever hospitals, tuberculosis hospitals and sanatoria, as well as children's hospitals for special ailments and for convalescents.

There are thirty-one special hospitals with a total bed accommodation in 1937 of 13,519.

These hospitals comprise:

Seventeen hospitals for infectious diseases, six hospitals for tuberculosis in adults, three hospitals for tuberculosis in children, and five children's hospitals.

Admission to the general hospitals can be obtained on the application of a doctor to the medical superintendent of the nearest hospital. For admission to a special hospital, application must be made to the Medical Officer of Health at the County Hall. Except in respect of tuberculosis and infectious diseases, which are treated free, patients are required to contribute what they can afford towards the cost of their maintenance and treatment.

During 1937 the number of in-patients who received treatment in the L.C.C. hospitals was:

General hospitals, 228,177 (including 19,218 live births).

Special hospitals, 55,737 (including 182 live births).

The number of out-patients who received treatment at the L.C.C. hospitals was 191,515 (including 21,510 antenatal patients).

The London Ambulance Service was established in 1915, primarily to deal with street accidents. In 1930, following the Local Government Act 1929, the ambulance service of the Metropolitan Asylums Board and the ambulance services maintained by the late Boards of Guardians were incorporated with the Council's service.

The service is now centralised at the County Hall, where a large telephone switch-board is installed, forming a miniature exchange through which all calls for ambulances are received.

There are six large ambulance stations each holding twenty-five vehicles and sixteen smaller stations each holding two ambulances.

There are 153 ambulances as well as a fleet of twenty ambulance omnibuses each holding from eighteen to twenty patients.

Ambulances are sent out from the large stations to deal with the removal of sick persons requiring hospital treatment. Those from the smaller stations deal with street accidents and all emergencies. Each ambulance is staffed by two men who are skilled drivers and possess adequate first-aid qualifications, and in many cases nurses accompany the patients. The staff consists of one officer in charge, one assistant officer, seven superintendents, eighteen ambulance station officers, and 379 drivers and attendants.

Ambulances are provided without charge for the removal of (i) all cases of accident, (ii) cases of sudden illness in public places, (iii) cases of life or death in private houses on the application of a doctor, (iv) maternity cases to hospitals, and (v) cases of infectious diseases.

Over 372,000 persons use the ambulances every year. The average time from the receipt of a call to an accident case to the arrival of the ambulance is 6¼ minutes.

The City of London maintains its own service.

All that you have to do in case of an accident in the County of London is to go to the nearest telephone and call "Ambulance", giving the place of the accident and the name of the caller. No charge is made.

If it is necessary to dial, you dial "999" and then ask for "Ambulance".

On the day of the Coronation thirty-eight ambulances were placed at different points of the route and 152 cases were dealt with. The total number of casualties dealt with during the day was 467, a record.

55,486 telephone calls were received in 1937. The ambulances cover over a quarter of a million miles in the year.

The average time from receipt of a call to arrival at the hospital for all stations in 1937 was just over 18 minutes.

The duty of promoting the welfare of the blind is also a function of the L.C.C.

In 1935 there were 6892 registered blind persons in the County of London, rather more than 10 per cent of all the registered blind persons in England and Wales. Of these 4862 were over fifty.

Blind children under school age are dealt with at Child Welfare centres and by visitation by health visitors. Children of school age come under the L.C.C. education authorities.

Boys and girls over sixteen are given technical training and employment in workshops, and after-care is provided for by the L.C.C. and voluntary agencies.

If the training institutions cannot provide employment the Board try to place him in another workshop or in a Home Worker's Scheme.

In 1935 there were 524 London blind persons employed in workshops for the blind, working at basket-making, bedding-making, brush-making, boot-repairing, chair-caning, quilting and weaving.

169 blind persons were accommodated in homes and sixty-three in hostels.

Thirty home teachers visited some 4067 blind people in their own homes to teach Braille and Moon and organise pastime and occupation centres.

If the death-rate from all causes of 1889–93 had persisted until 1933–37 there would have been 424,866 deaths in London during the latter period of five years. In fact, they numbered only 255,519, and on this basis 169,347 lives were saved during the five years, or 33,869 each year.

Similarly, the campaign against infectious disease has resulted in a great saving of lives: for example, if the 1889–93 death-rate from typhoid fever had persisted there would have been 2765 deaths in the quinquennium 1933–37, whereas there were actually only 105. In the case of measles the number of deaths would have been 12,360 as against 1583 actually recorded in the last five years, although the drop in the birth-rate is also partly responsible for this; and the deaths from scarlet fever numbered 4902 (1889–93) as compared with 251 (1933–37). This shows that for these three diseases alone 18,088 lives have been saved in the last five years or an average of 3618 a year.

The deaths of infants 0–1 on the basis of the rate for 1889–93 would have numbered 43,558, whereas they were actually 17,438, showing a saving of 26,120 lives in the five years or an annual average of 5224.

These figures are of course included in the total number of deaths from all causes mentioned above in the first paragraph.

The outstanding feature of L.C.C. hospitals during 1937 was the work done for maternity purposes.

1938 saw the largest number of births and the smallest number of maternal deaths yet recorded. The births totalled 19,944 compared with 18,261 in 1936 and 15,519 in 1935.

The rate for maternal deaths fell from 4·9 per 1000

births in 1933 to 1·58 in 1937. For patients who had antenatal care in the Council's clinics the rate is now only 1 per
1000.

In accordance with its policy of removing the hospitals
from the scope of the Poor Law the Council had "appropriated" three more hospitals, and there were now under
the Council's control forty-four general hospitals and institutions, containing 22,309 beds, and thirty-one special
hospitals with 13,519 beds, making a total bed accommodation of 35,828. And this is apart from beds in the
mental hospitals.

Mental Health Services

I hope that the words "lunatic", "asylum" and "pauper"
are unfamiliar to you.

Indeed they ought to be because they have all been
abolished by Act of Parliament.

But evil words have a nasty knack of sticking, and most
of us have shivered with horror reading of the treatment
meted out to the poor mentally afflicted patients of the past.

Progress in civilisation is slow, but there is progress.
Lunatics have been laughed at and lunatics have been
worshipped, but only in recent years have they been
treated as patients suffering from a curable malady.

Asylums have been converted into mental hospitals and
the change is much more than a change in name.

The L.C.C. Mental Health services combine two distinct services, those dealing (a) with mental disorder and
(b) with mental deficiency.

There is a vast difference between these two types of
mental malady and each requires a quite different treatment.

People of unsound mind are those who after an apparently normal childhood develop a derangement or a dis-

ordered conduct, whereas mental defectives are those who have never developed up to normal limits. Their development is what is called "arrested".

Do not confuse "arrested" with "retarded".

Some of the most brilliant men who have ever lived seemed to their parents and teachers unnaturally stupid in youth. This was simply because they developed slowly. "Arrested" development means development that stops altogether. Those who suffer from mental disorder need remedial treatment, which aims at restoring the patient to completely normal mental health.

Mental defectives, on the other hand, are trained to improve their conduct, their self-reliance and self-control up to a pitch that will enable them to occupy a place of some usefulness in society, if not a very exalted place.

Mentally disordered patients are dealt with under the Lunacy and Mental Treatment Acts 1890–1930.

Under the Lunacy Act 1890 the L.C.C. is charged with the duty of providing and maintaining mental hospitals for rate-aided patients and it may provide accommodation for private paying patients.

Under the Mental Treatment Act 1930 a great step forward was provided by the opportunity then given for the first time to patients to present themselves voluntarily for treatment at any public mental hospital.

Temporary treatment is provided without certification for six months, which may be extended to twelve, for patients who are for the time incapable of expressing willingness or unwillingness to receive such treatment.

Mental defectives are dealt with under the Mental Deficiency Act 1913, amended in 1927.

It is the duty of the L.C.C. to find out what persons in its area are mentally defective from birth or early age and to provide one of three recognised forms of care.

They can have supervision in their own home, care in

a certified institution, or be placed under the guardianship of a private person.

The finding of mentally defective school children lies in the hands of the school medical service.

The L.C.C. maintains twenty-one institutions for the care of London's mentally afflicted.

These institutions contain in all 33,823 beds, and are divided up in the following order:

Hospitals for nervous and mental disorders (certified, voluntary and temporary patients)

Banstead Hospital, Sutton.
Bexley Hospital, Bexley.
Cane Hill Hospital, Coulsdon.
Claybury Hospital, Woodford Bridge.
Friern Hospital, New Southgate.
Horton Hospital, Epsom.
Long Grove Hospital, Epsom.
St Bernard's Hospital, Southall.
St Ebba's Hospital, Epsom.
West Park Hospital, Epsom.

Hospital for nervous and mental disorders (voluntary patients only)

Maudsley Hospital, Denmark Hill.

Institutions for the mentally defective

Brunswick House, Mistley.
Darenth Park, Dartford.
Farmfield, Horley.
Fountain Hospital, Tooting.
The Manor, Epsom.
South Side Home, Streatham.

Institutions accommodating chronic harmless persons of unsound mind and mentally defectives

Caterham Hospital, Caterham.
Leavesden Hospital, Abbots Langley.

Hospital for aged persons suffering from senile dementia

Tooting Bec Hospital, Tooting Bec.

Patients who have become mentally disordered after sleeping sickness are concentrated at West Park, and those who have suffered from general paralysis of the insane are treated with induced malaria at Horton.

Very strict classification is observed in mental hospitals.

The patient enters a special unit, which may be completely detached from the rest of the hospital, and is there closely observed. Indeed the whole of his time may be spent in the admission unit without ever having to associate with the less hopeful cases.

This unit serves as a sorting centre from which patients can be distributed to other special units.

Turbulent patients with a tendency to suicide, epileptics, chronic, irrecoverable but quiet patients and those recovering are all classified in their own special sections, so that so far as possible uncongenial cases do not come into contact with each other more closely than can be helped.

Accommodation is carried out in many instances in detached villas. St Ebba's is built entirely on the villa system.

Mental defectives are graded, trainable cases being treated at the Manor and Darenth Park, where industrial training is carried out. Hostels are attached to each of these where mentally defective girls are trained for local domestic service.

At Brunswick House male defectives are trained in farming. At South Side House girls are trained for domestic service and at Farmfield there is special provision for criminals and intractables.

Low-grade defectives are sent to Caterham, or if infirm to Leavesden. The Fountain Hospital is confined to children of low mental grade.

Out of every ten patients admitted to the L.C.C. mental

hospitals during the last five years three could be discharged as recovered, of whom, on an average, one relapsed and was readmitted.

This is a vast improvement on the previous five years.

During 1937, 2720 patients were admitted and 843 recovered. These do not include voluntary patients.

One of the most interesting curative experiments is that carried out at Horton, where *anopheles* mosquitoes are bred and infected for the transmission of malaria to general paralytic patients.

It has been found that if they get malaria a considerable proportion of these paralytics recover. Indeed, seventy-four out of 136 cases recovered in 1937. As general paralysis was formerly considered to be fatal this is a great step forward.

Many patients in mental hospitals suffer from "dementia precox" or "schizophrenia".

It was discovered that shocks induced either by rapid arousing from a coma by large doses of insulin or by the injection of a camphor compound known as cardiazol did much to restore the patient to normality.

Since June 1937 cardiazol treatment has been tried at all the suitable hospitals, including the Maudsley. It is estimated that 16 per cent have recovered and a further 46 per cent improved since June 1937.

Patients gain confidence and strength in assisting with the domestic work, in the farms and in workshops, where they learn tailoring, bootmaking and so on.

Self-centred and listless patients benefit very much from manual occupation, even the apparently hopeless cases occupying their hands in sorting wool and other semi-automatic work.

In institutions for the mentally defective provision is

made for healthy occupations and recreations for minds that have never functioned completely.

Industry is the keynote.

Its first business is to shelter from the outside world those who by reason of feeble intellect cannot take their place in it, but it is not content to be merely a refuge. It aims at developing them into capable wage earners.

About 10 per cent prove to be suitable for leave of absence with a view to ultimate discharge.

The scout and guide movement is adopted in five of the institutions with very happy results.

Psychiatric social workers keep in close touch with the patients when they return to the outer world and help them to face it.

Mentally disordered patients are allowed the greatest possible freedom consistent with their own and the public safety, many of them being allowed parole either within or outside the institution estate. Walking parties are organised and groups are taken to local entertainments.

Mentally defective patients may be allowed leave of absence up to seven days and sometimes longer. In the summer they are often taken to the sea.

Indeed, every effort is made to provide for the patient as much recreation and amusement as possible in order to give the utmost variety.

All the large mental institutions are fitted out with recreation halls, in which concerts and films and dances take place regularly, and billiards and whist drives are also frequently played.

Outdoor games and physical drill are very popular, and the summer outdoor fête held at each institution is one of the most eagerly awaited events of the year.

Patients are at liberty to spend their pocket money at the canteens.

Special care is taken to give them suitable diet served under the most cheerful conditions at small tables holding four or eight patients.

They are encouraged to dress as they would dress at home and to introduce as colourful a note as possible.

By far the most remarkable of the hospitals is the Maudsley Hospital.

Dr Henry Maudsley, a famous psychiatrist, gave £30,000 to the L.C.C. in 1908, and £10,000 later by bequest, to establish a special hospital for the early treatment of cases of recoverable mental disorder. It should also be a centre for teaching and research.

It was here that voluntary patients were first allowed in England fifteen years before the Act of 1930.

Patients have never been received under orders for compulsory detention.

Of the 980 cases treated in 1937, 50 per cent were discharged as recovered or relieved.

Additional accommodation will provide for children suffering from mental and nervous disturbance.

Voluntary patients are received at the L.C.C. mental hospitals, especially at St Ebba's, which is now acting as second string to the Maudsley.

The Mental After Care Association finds employment for discharged patients, makes grants of money, supplies clothes and provides convalescent homes.

About 400 mental defectives are placed under the guardianship of responsible people.

Some 3500 well-behaved, employable, middle and high-grade defectives who have no homes or unsatisfactory ones are now being placed under the guardianship of the Council's own officers, living in lodgings with selected families.

Training is given in occupation and craft centres in

games, physical exercises and handicrafts. Attendance is purely voluntary.

The responsibility of caring for 34,000 mentally afflicted persons is very heavy.

All the necessities of life have to be provided for them and particularly sympathy with their distress. To cure the sickness of the mind and to make the sufferers happy if they cannot be cured, and to train the mentally deficient to become more useful, these are services of the highest order and the L.C.C. is tackling the problem of the mentally afflicted with characteristic vigour and thoroughness.

Chapter 11   LONDON'S BLIND

Before 1920 the welfare of all blind people was in the hands
of voluntary organisations, but by the Blind Persons Act
1920 all blind people became eligible for old Age Pensions
at fifty and every county and borough authority was held
responsible for the welfare of the blind in its area.

The L.C.C. decided not to provide or maintain new
institutions for the blind but to avail itself of the existing
institutions.

Up to 1930 the main supervision of the services for the
blind was carried out by the Ministry of Health. But the
Local Government Act of 1929 transferred these functions
to county authorities.

The Blind Persons Act 1938 reduced the age at which the
blind could claim Old Age Pensions from fifty to forty,
and made it compulsory to remove blind persons from the
scope of the poor law.

The definition of blindness under this act is "so blind as to be unable to perform any work for which eyesight is essential".

Before receiving any benefit the person has to be examined and certified as blind by one of the Council's ophthalmologists.

On 31 March 1938 there were 7460 blind people in London, 5090 of them being unemployable, living in their own homes or private lodgings.

Under the Education Act of 1921, elementary and secondary education are provided for blind children up to the age of sixteen.

The girls are educated at Elm Court School, West Norwood, and the boys at Linden Lodge, Bolingbroke Grove, Battersea.

The definition of blindness for a child is "too blind to be able to read the ordinary school books read by children".

On leaving school blind children are given the chance of learning the trades of basket-making, bedding-making and upholstery, boot repairing, brush-making, chair caning, knitting, knitting-needle-making, mat-making, and soap-making. The training for these trades occupies from one to four years.

There are workshops for blind persons where each worker gets 15s. supplementary pay in addition to the standard wage.

The income of blind persons may be augmented, by domiciliary assistance, to 27s. 6d. a week for the head of the house, 25s. to others; blind married couples to 45s. a week and married couples, one of whom is blind, to 45s. a week.

£125,000 was spent on domiciliary assistance for the blind in 1937–38.

Four branch offices of the welfare of the blind are now

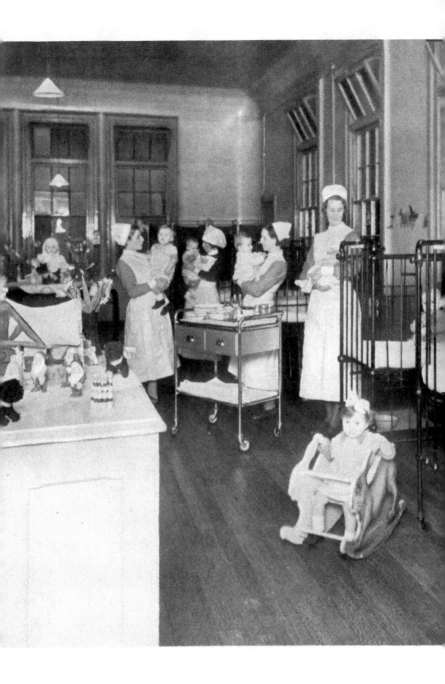

Public Assistance Institution nursery

High Wood Hospital

established and a staff of thirty-seven have visitors employed who teach the handicrafts of basketry, chair caning, hand knitting, raffia and sea grass work, rugmaking, rush mats and seating.

About 120,000 visits were paid by L.C.C. officers to the blind in 1938.

Ten pastime, occupation and social centres are attended by more than 700 blind persons, where the same handicrafts are encouraged and a high degree of skill is acquired.

The Postmaster-General grants a free wireless licence to any registered blind person not resident in a school.

The National Library for the Blind provides and distributes literature and music to the blind and receives an annual grant from the L.C.C. of £840.

The maintenance votes for the care and welfare of the blind have risen from £1000 in 1922–23 to £99,635 for 1934–35 and £228,640 for 1938–39. This excludes the £14,000 spent on training the blind and the cost of maintaining them in hospitals and institutions.

Of this £228,640, £172,000 is spent on domiciliary assistance, and £25,000 on workshop employees.

Chapter 12   LONDON'S FIRE BRIGADE

We are always reading of towns being burnt down in the Middle Ages, and London was no exception.

So long as houses were built of wood and thatched with straw fires were bound to be widespread, and the steps taken to put these fires out were quite inadequate.

In 1135, for instance, a fire broke out at London Bridge, destroyed St Paul's Cathedral and only stopped at St Clement Danes because there were no more houses to catch fire.

Some fifty-four years later the first mayor of London promulgated a "First Assize of Buildings" encouraging the use of stone instead of wood.

And when in 1212 London Bridge was again burnt down and many lives were lost in the noblemen's houses that were gutted, a "Second Assize" was passed demanding that all new houses should be roofed with tiles, shingles, boards or lead in place of reeds and rushes.

Every alderman had to "keep a crook and cord", and vessels filled with water were supposed to be placed before every door.

And that is about all the protection against fire that the Londoner bothered about or got until the Great Fire of 1666 taught him how ill-equipped he was to fight the fire menace.

Buckets, hand squirts and a few pumps and ladders were not much use against fire on a scale like that. Moreover, water was scarce, and the pipes of the new River Company were found to be dry.

The only thing that proved of any value was to blow up buildings to form gaps in the path of the fire too wide for the flames to cross.

In 1668 the City was divided into four districts, each of which had to be supplied with 800 leather buckets, 50 ladders from 16 to 42 feet long, "As many hand squirts of brass as will furnish two for every parish", 24 pickaxe sledges and 40 shod shovels. Each of the twelve principal City companies had to provide 30 buckets, 1 "engine", 6 pickaxe sledges, 3 ladders and 2 hand squirts of brass. The engine may have been a hand squirt mounted on a cistern.

Then from 1680 onwards came the foundation of the Fire Insurance Companies.

And at the beginning these companies not only paid the insurers but extinguished the fires themselves. They dressed their firemen or "watermen", as they were sometimes called, in livery and gave them badges, and the insured premises had "firemarks" fixed on their walls as a guide to the firemen and to prevent fraudulent claims against the companies.

These watermen were exempt from being seized for the Navy by the press gang.

In 1707 an Act was passed making it compulsory for every London parish to keep one large fire engine and one hand engine.

The local churchwardens were responsible for fixing fire-cocks on water-mains and pipes in their parishes and for the placing of marks (forerunners of our hydrant tablets) on houses to show their position.

In 1774 a further Act decreed that every parish should provide three or more ladders of one, two and three storeys high to help people to escape from burning houses.

But as late as the beginning of the last century London had to depend on private brigades kept by the insurance companies, who naturally only put out fires insured by their company, and a good deal of confusion followed on the rivalry between the insurance companies and the parish brigades.

In 1832 ten companies joined to form the London Fire Engine Establishment with James Braidwood, who had been in command of the Edinburgh Fire Brigade, as superintendent.

Four years later, a voluntary organisation, the Royal Society for the Protection of Life from Fire, came into being and supplemented the work of the Fire Engine Establishment and the parochial brigades by manning fire escapes at a number of stations in central London.

But the Great Tooley Street fire of 1861, in which Mr Braidwood lost his life, showed how inadequate the fire-fighting forces were. In addition to the loss of many lives this fire entailed a loss of about £2,000,000.

This decided the Government to place the responsibility for the protection of London from fire upon the Metropolitan Board of Works.

So in 1866 the Board took over the equipment and staff of the Fire Engine Establishment and the parish fire

engines and in the following year took over the eighty-five
escapes and staff of the Society for the Protection of Life
from Fire. A tablet commemorating the taking over of the
insurance companies' brigade has recently been presented
by their successors and can be seen in the entrance hall of
the new headquarters.

The first chief of the Metropolitan Fire Brigade was
Captain (later Sir) Eyre Massey Shaw, who, in addition
to commanding the brigade with distinction for thirty
years, became a well-known public figure and was carica-
tured in *Vanity Fair* and immortalised by Gilbert and
Sullivan in *Iolanthe*.

On the back of a cartoon by "Ape" of this very popular
figure runs this entertaining description:

MEN OF THE DAY. NO. 24

Captain Eyre Shaw

Captain Shaw is so much the fireman of London that
he is the first thorough fireman we have had in a city which
requires one, perhaps, more than any other in the world.
He has organised the Metropolitan Fire Brigade so in-
telligently, and with such completeness, that it is now in-
comparably the best force of that kind existing in any
country; and with a network of electric telegraphs all over
London, he can from his office despatch all the engines in
the town to a fire in two, or at most three minutes after it
has first been reported and in a quarter of an hour more
would be throwing tons of water upon the flames.

When, a few days ago, the news arrived that Paris was
burning, Captain Shaw, with the readiness that dis-
tinguishes him, offered at once to take over his best engines
and a large body of his men, with whom he could have
dealt with the fire in a way that would have astonished

the wretched Parisian pompiers. His offer was at first gratefully accepted; and when the French Government changed its mind about the necessity for further help, Jules Favre telegraphed his thanks for the aid offered in terms which are the latest, though not the highest, tribute made to Captain Shaw's eminence in his profession. He is, besides being the first fireman, one of the most popular men in London and he well deserves his popularity.

In 1878 the headquarters were transferred from Watling Street to a new station in Southwark Bridge Road.

The Brigade was maintained (i) by a halfpenny rate on all rateable property, (ii) by contributions by the fire insurance companies at the rate of £35 per million pounds of the amounts insured by them and (iii) by £10,000 a year contributed by the Government. The limitation on the rate was abolished in 1888 when the London County Council was formed and took over the Brigade. For sixteen years it was still called the Metropolitan Fire Brigade, but in 1904 its name was changed to London Fire Brigade.

In 1893 the first sliding escape was introduced, and in 1897 Captain Wells, the then Chief Officer, introduced a horsed escape in which the escape could be slipped while the van was travelling.

Then in 1906 came the first motor escape vans.

The first steam fire engines in England were built in 1829. In 1855 came the first boat specially built and fitted out as a floating steam engine, although fire vessels with hand pumps had probably been in use since 1760. It was not until 1860 that a steam fire engine was used on land in London.

Originally the fire vessels used on the river were too large to be used at low tide, so they had to be replaced by tug boats drawing only a few feet of water and towing land pumping engines on rafts.

The first modern fire boat, the *Alpha II* with a steam engine fuelled by coal, was introduced in 1900. As it had a draught of less than 2 feet it was able to navigate the river at all states of the tide.

During the war the Brigade was severely tested, particularly in the summer of 1917, by a series of air raids. There were in all twenty-five air raids on London, almost all starting fires, but in only six of them were the fires serious. Much valuable work was also done in bringing people out from collapsed buildings.

The last horse-drawn escape was withdrawn in 1920 and the last horse-drawn vehicle, a turntable ladder, was withdrawn in the following year. The mechanisation of the Brigade made it possible to close fifteen stations without altering the principle that appliances shall be on the scene of a fire in any part of the County within five minutes and that at least a hundred men shall be available within fifteen minutes.

Until 1920 all Members of the Brigade were accommodated in quarters attached to or in the actual station and were available for duty for the whole twenty-four hours.

In 1920 a two-shift system was introduced enabling firemen and sub-officers to live where they pleased on a rent allowance.

In 1934 came the dual-purpose appliance, which carries a 50-foot escape as well as a standard fire pump. To-day there are 128 pumping appliances, and a 40-foot extension ladder is now carried on each pump for use in forecourts, back gardens and areas where it is not possible to take the wheeled escape.

The dual purpose appliances at twenty-eight key stations are always kept available.

A new fire boat, the *Massey Shaw*, commissioned in 1935, did very useful work at the great fire at Colonial Wharf, Wapping, in the same year. It is 78 feet long, equipped with eight deck deliveries and a monitor capable of projecting a heavy stream of water in any direction. It has a pumping capacity of 3000 gallons a minute at a pressure of 100 lb. per square inch. It can navigate the river at every state of the tide.

The first enclosed pump was introduced in 1933. It gives the crew complete protection in all weathers.

All the wooden turntable ladders have now been replaced by 100 foot all-steel ladders mounted on chassis with pneumatic tyres.

The old shining brass helmets have been replaced, except for ceremonial purposes, by a new helmet of cork and rubber which affords the firemen far more protection, particularly against electric shocks, and are lighter and more comfortable to wear for long periods.

The headquarters of the Fire Brigade was changed from Southwark Bridge Road in 1937 to the present magnificent buildings, the chief of which is a ten-storey block 100 feet high and over 200 feet long on the Albert Embankment.

This block contains the fire-station with seven run-outs on the ground floor, and accommodation for the firemen, administrative offices and residential quarters on the upper floors.

There is a tiled drill-yard at the back with a brick-faced drill tower 100 feet high at one end and a bandstand at the other.

On the other side of Lambeth High Street is a four-storey building with garage on the ground floor and the Brigade Training School above. Behind this come the workshops and the stores. The cost of the site, buildings and equipment was £389,000.

The old Tooting Fire Station (*left*) and Fire Brigade Headquarters to-day

A fire on the wharf

In the main entrance hall are panels giving a list of the sixty-two officers and men of the Fire Brigade who in the last hundred years have given up their lives to save others. Their memorial is a bronze and marble depiction of a modern fire-fighting scene and it was presented by the underwriters of Lloyd's.

In the floor is a mosaic depicting the Fire of London.

In the appliance room, which has seven run-outs, are a dual-purpose appliance, a pump, a turntable ladder, an emergency tender, a breakdown lorry, a hose lorry and a canteen van.

Electric immersion heaters make the starting-up of the engines instantaneous.

In the museum are two old steam fire-engines, one still in working order after fifty-four years' service, and a manual fire-engine over 200 years old, complete with leather hose and branch. James Braidwood's leather helmet and the helmet and axe of Sir Eyre Massey Shaw are also preserved as well as a fine collection of fire-marks.

On the first floor is the "sound-proofed" control room, from which radiate private lines in duplicate to each of the six superintendent stations and the Divisional Station at Euston, the home of the Northern Divisional officer. There are special lines to County Hall, the London Salvage Corps, and Ambulance Headquarters, and exchange lines for administrative purposes. There is a self-contained emergency lighting system both for the control room and watch room below, so that even if the main electricity supply fails there will be no interruption of activities.

Accommodation is provided on the first floor for all sub-officers and firemen on duty. Men on night shift are allowed to rest from 10 p.m. to 6.45 a.m. when not required for duty and there is a recreation room with two billiard tables.

The second and third floors are occupied by members of the administrative and technical staff.

From the fourth floor upward are the quarters of the officers, for whom a squash rackets court is provided in the rear block.

The water for drill and displays comes from three underground tanks and two hydrants. The 100 foot drill-tower has its upper storeys set back to provide terraces and it is the first drill tower in the brigade with an internal staircase. The body of the tower is adapted for the drying of hose and can accommodate over sixty 100 foot lengths. The air in the tower can be warmed artificially and there is an electrically driven hoist to lift the wet hose to the top.

Next to the tower is a hose-testing plant. Selected lengths of all rubber-lined hose are tested on delivery to an internal pressure of 400 lb. per square inch, and periodically to 150 lb. per square inch.

On the river opposite the main buildings is a pier with a pontoon alongside which a fire boat is moored.

Every Wednesday afternoon throughout the year a public drill display is given, admission is free and tickets are to be obtained by writing to the Chief Officer at least a fortnight before the day.

I attended the display given on the Wednesday before Guy Fawkes' Day, which incidentally is always the worst day of the year in London for outbreaks of fire.

As I was being led upstairs to my seat on the balcony I heard the very stirring "L.F.B. and L.A.F.S. March", specially composed by Sir Walford Davies, being played by the Fire Brigade Band.

I was surprised to find practically every seat all round

the building occupied and most of them by boys and girls who had come in groups from the schools.

The show began on the stroke of three o'clock with a drill that caused a good deal of amusement.

A squad of sixteen men marched into the drill yard, grounded and unrolled sheets, after which one man lay flat while his opposite number turned him over, flung him over his right shoulder and marched off.

The rescued feigned the limpness of the insensible with such dramatic intensity that a roar of delighted laughter went up at the sight of the row of loosely swaying capless heads.

The next turn was a demonstration of the use of a first-aid appliance in putting out a very actively burning wood-stack.

Then came the extinction of a petrol fire.

As the great yellow flames rose high Commander Firebrace asked me to guess how long this would take.

Knowing the extraordinary efficiency of the Fire Brigade I said: "Ten seconds."

He laughed.

"We're not quite such miracle workers as that. Say forty-five."

But it turned out that I was right. It took just ten seconds.

After this we watched a man cutting his way by oxy-acetylene through an iron bar and a man stood fully masked with special oxygen-breathing apparatus.

Then came one of the great thrills of the afternoon.

Recruits gave an exhibition of climbing to the top of the 100 foot tower with hook-ladders light enough for them to hand up from storey to storey and firmly enough fixed for them to climb.

This is not a demonstration that I should like to have

taken part in, for from a distance there seemed all too little for the ladders to cling on to, but I was assured that in skilled hands they were a safe and efficient means of scaling a building.

There was comic relief in the display given by men pushing up and down the handles of a manual fire-engine accompanied by a succession of "Hi's" and other loud cries, and loud laughter greeted the excellent acting of the man who appeared at an upper window of the tower among flames and smoke crying "Help! Help!" He darted so excitedly along the window-sill that I expected to see him fall at any second.

He ran from floor to floor and was eventually found "unconscious" on the top floor and sent rapidly down into the yard on a rope. He looked very much like a man being saved at sea on a breeches buoy.

I was beginning to see why there was a strongly Naval atmosphere and influence about the Fire Brigade.

A fireman's job is very like a sailor's in having to get used to climbing great heights, and being continually preoccupied with water.

One of the jolliest of all sights was that of two firemen standing on the top of steel turntable ladders and being propelled automatically higher and higher until they both came to rest opposite the eighth storey of the tower and vigorously plied the open window with water.

Finally, we went down to the main hall and watched the despatch of appliances from all seven run-outs.

The excitement of watching the brass helmeted firemen standing precariously on horse-drawn red fire engines tearing frantically along the streets to the alarming tune of the fire bell has given place to excitement of a more efficient sort. The sight may not be so colourful, but the smooth functionings of the modern appliances more than make up for that. The object of a fire brigade is to save life and property and time is the essential factor to be considered.

The Fire Brigade is probably the most spectacular of all the activities of the L.C.C. and in consequence it is the one about which the general public knows most.

Its publicity methods might well be copied by other departments.

K-S

Chapter 13   LONDON'S PROTECTION

It was in 1891 that the L.C.C. formed for the first time a Public Control Committee.

It had authority to exercise the powers of the Council under Acts dealing with explosives, infant life protection, weights and measures, and the testing of gas and gas meters.

All questions relating to coroners and coroners' courts in the County of London were referred to them and they were responsible for duties connected with the supply of water in the County and for the prevention of nuisance from smoke.

They were further given powers to conduct enquiries relating to markets and market rights in London and entrusted with animal diseases.

They still carry out all these services, except those concerned with the water supply, prevention of smoke nuisance and infant life protection.

They also now deal with revenue collection and the registration of motor vehicles.

The title "Public Control" suggests police, but it really means protection and help.

Control in the L.C.C. sense means seeing that citizens' lives are not endangered or their health impaired by avoidable nuisances.

The only members of the public who are controlled in the sense of restrained are those who attempt to exploit, cheat, or do injury to their fellow-citizens, or who by their actions place the lives and properties of others in danger.

It is found that Londoners are generally ready to help all the L.C.C. control inspectors to carry out their variegated tasks. Here are some of the jobs they are called upon to tackle.

Carbide of Calcium. Licences are granted for the storage of carbide of calcium, which is usually kept for the generation of acetylene in flare lamps and generators used in connection with oxy-acetylene welding and cutting. 458 licences were granted by the L.C.C. in 1937.

Celluloid. Following upon a number of serious celluloid fires between 1902 and 1912, an Act was passed requiring premises where celluloid or cinematograph film was stored to be registered.

Celluloid may not be stored in any part of a building under another part that is used as a residence, and adequate means of escape must be provided.

The L.C.C. has, however, no control over the storage of manufactured celluloid articles or the keeping of film for private use.

Coroners. The L.C.C. is responsible for the appointment of coroners, the payment of their salaries and expenses and the provision of inquest accommodation.

Once he is appointed, however, the L.C.C. have no

control over the way in which he carries out his duties and they cannot dismiss him.

They have twice appealed to the Lord Chancellor for the removal of coroners but without success.

In the old days inquests were held in public-houses.

In 1894 no less than 568 inquests were held in inns, but this practice was then suppressed and no inquest has been held in an inn since 1901.

Diseases of Animals. This part of the Public Control activities is dwindling.

In 1889–1900, 2763 cases of animal diseases were dealt with by Control Inspectors, whereas in 1936–37 only thirteen cases were dealt with.

There has been no case of rabies since 1889, and very few cases of foot and mouth disease are ever notified in London.

The number of animals kept in London is diminishing very rapidly.

One of the Inspector's chief duties now is the inspection of animals brought to London for slaughter.

During 1937, 37,911 cattle, 20,386 sheep and 38,274 pigs were examined.

Under the Agriculture Act of 1937 the L.C.C. has now ceased to be responsible for the veterinary work arising under the Diseases of Animals Act.

Employment Agencies. In 1905 the L.C.C. obtained powers to register all agencies for domestic servants, and for certain agencies for concert, variety and theatrical artistes.

A scheme for legalising the annual licensing of agencies came into force in 1910 and this was extended to dancing schools.

Agencies are now prohibited from charging more than 2s. 6d. as a preliminary fee.

In 1937 there were over 1000 licensed employment agencies dealing with servants, governesses, nurses, actors (film and stage), salesmen, clerks, waiters, chefs and so on.

Explosives. Control over the manufacture, storage, sale and conveyance of explosives is dealt with under the Explosives Act of 1875.

In 1937, 4600 premises were registered with the L.C.C. to keep fireworks and (or) gunpowder.

Local Taxation Licences. The levying of the duty on local taxation licences was transferred from the Commissioners of Customs and Excise to the L.C.C. in 1909.

These licences, which are now limited to the keeping of dogs, using or wearing of armorial bearings, carrying guns and killing and dealing in game, are issued at Post Offices and by the Council, to whom the whole of the revenue goes.

Massage Establishments. All massage, chiropodists, manicurists and beauty parlours have to be registered.

In 1937, 2990 of these were licensed in London.

Performing Animals. All persons exhibiting performing animals have to be registered, and officers are authorised to inspect premises where animals are trained or exhibited.

Petroleum Oil and Spirit. Licences have to be obtained to keep petrol and 5400 premises are now registered; the amount of spirit exceeds 11½ million gallons kept at any one time.

The object of these licences is to prevent the occurrence of fire.

Road Fund Licences. The L.C.C. issues licences of drivers in London and there are more than a million names on the Council's register.

Over 50,000 certificates for new drivers have been issued since 1935.

In 1921, 131,541 car licences were issued in London; in 1937, 593,660 licences were granted.

The registration of motors enables the ownership of any vehicle to be traced almost at once.

Sale of Gas. There are seventeen testing places within the County where the calorific values and the pressures of the gas are continuously and automatically recorded.

Three offices are maintained for the testing of gas meters and every year about 300,000 recently repaired meters are examined.

Shops Act. Up to 1912 all that legislation had done was to compel the provision of seats for the use of female shop assistants and make it illegal for anybody under eighteen years of age to work for more than 74 hours a week.

The Shops Act 1912 made it compulsory for every assistant to have one half holiday every week and that shops should shut at 1 o'clock on one day in the week. Reasonable intervals had to be allowed for meals.

During the war under the Defence of the Realm Act, usually called "D.O.R.A.", shops had to be shut at certain specified hours in the evening. In 1928 it was replaced by the Shops (Hours of Closing) Act, which decided that 8 p.m. should be the usual closing hour and 9 p.m. on one day of the week.

In 1934 a further Shops Act reduced the maximum hours that a young person should be employed to 48, and from 1 January 1940 these hours will be reduced to 44 for all people under sixteen, who in addition are not permitted to work overtime.

Except in special circumstances no shop assistant under eighteen may be employed after 10 p.m. or before 6 a.m.

Shops have to satisfy the requirements of the Act about

Fire in the City

Above: Galloping to the rescue—the old Fire Brigade
Below: A modern fire engine

lighting, ventilation and temperature and the provision of adequate lavatories.

The Metropolitan Borough Councils have to see that the sanitary conveniences, ventilation and temperature are of the required standard.

Van boys, errand boys and street traders are also protected by the Act, and by a new Act—the Young Persons (Employment) Act 1938—certain other young persons who are not shop assistants are similarly protected from 1 January 1939. Among these are office boys in newspaper offices, and page boys in hotels and cinemas. Under the Shops (Sunday Trading Restriction) Act 1936 all shops, except a certain type, are required to be closed on Sundays. Shop assistants who work on Sundays have a holiday during the week, and if they work for more than four hours on Sunday, they are not allowed to work more than three Sundays in the same month.

Certain areas are allowed to keep shops open till 2 o'clock on Sunday afternoon. Petticoat Lane is the most famous of these.

Another aspect of Public Control is

Treasure trove. Do you know what treasure trove is? Here is its definition:

"Treasure trove is where any gold or silver, in coin, plate or bullion is found concealed in a house, or in the earth, or in a private place, the owner thereof being unknown, in which case the treasure belongs to the King; but if he who laid it down be known or afterwards discovered, the owner and not the King is entitled to it."

If the owner instead of hiding it, casually lost it or purposely parted with it, in such a manner that he intended to abandon the property altogether, and did not propose to resume ownership on another occasion, as if he threw it on the ground, or other public place or into the river, the first finder is entitled to the property against everyone except the owner—so it is the hiding and not the abandonment of the property that entitles the King to it.

A coroner has to summon a jury when the finding of any treasure becomes known and then asks them whether the find consisted of precious or base metal, where it was deposited, whether it was intentionally hidden or concealed or accidentally lost or purposely abandoned, whether the owner was known, who found it, and whether he concealed his find. If he did, so far from getting a reward he may be sent to prison.

If the coroner finds it to be treasure trove, he "seizes it for the King" and hands it over to the Treasury.

In December 1937 several gold coins of the reigns of James I and Charles I were discovered by two labourers as they were digging a draining trench.

The coins were sent to the British Museum and the finders were paid the value of the treasure less 20 per cent.

The Public Control department act as overseers of *Weights and Measures*.

You know the length of a foot, but do you know the length of a *span*? It is the length that can be spanned between the thumb-tip and the little-finger-tip of the outstretched hand.

The *palm* is the breadth of four fingers. The *digit* is the finger's breadth at about the middle of the middle finger. The *cubit* is the length of the bent forearm from elbow point to finger-tip. In 1266 it was decided that the English penny, called a sterling, should weigh 32 grains of wheat, well dried. 20 pence made an ounce, and 12 ounces made a pound.

In 1878 the Weights and Measures Act was passed and new standards made.

The yard is the unit measure of length, and the pound the unit measure of weight.

The Imperial standard yard is a bronze bar 1 square inch in section and 38 inches long. Near to each end a hole is sunk, the distance between the centres of the two holes being 36 inches.

The Imperial standard avoirdupois pound is a platinum cylinder about 1·35 inches deep and 1·15 inches in diameter.

These standards are kept in a dust-proof, fire-proof safe at a constant temperature of 62°.

Several copies have been made, which are compared with each other every ten years. The L.C.C. is called upon to provide local standards, which are compared by the Board of Trade with the reference standards and used by inspectors of weights and measures for comparing their working standards which they use to check weights and measures in use for trade.

The L.C.C. has divided the County into eighteen districts and appointed in each district an inspector of weights and measures. Seven coal officers are also employed to see that the weights of coal and coke are accurate.

When the inspector is satisfied he places his mark of approval or stamp on the weight, measure or weighing machine. If any trader uses a weight, measure or weighing machine which is not stamped he is liable to prosecution. The L.C.C. inspectors inspect about 2½ million weighing and measuring appliances every year. The appliances vary from a balance which will weigh a single hair to the weighbridge of 160 tons, from the automatic weigher of a ship's cargo of grain to the measurer of a milk bottle.

Up till 1926 the public was only protected against short weight in the sale of coal, bread and tea.

In that year an Act was passed making it a punishable

offence to sell short weight of any article of food or drink. In 1929 petrol pumps were required to be tested and stamped by inspectors.

The L.C.C. also protects the public in the sale of fertilisers and feeding stuffs for cattle and poultry. Inspectors take samples and see that these products contain the correct proportions of oils, phosphates, nitrogen, potash and so on.

One of the worst nuisances in London is caused by smoke and fog, which affects the health and delays the traffic, causing a tremendous loss in business.

Coal first came into use in London at the end of the thirteenth century, and its use became general as wood became more expensive. The smoke given off was considered so bad for health that in the reigns of Edward I and Elizabeth it was forbidden to use coal in London while Parliament was sitting.

In 1648 Londoners asked Parliament to prohibit the importation of coal from Newcastle, but it was not until 1845 that a law was passed requiring locomotive engines to be so constructed as to consume their own smoke.

Then a staff of fifty police constables was specially appointed to enforce certain restrictions about smoke from furnaces in factories, bath and wash-houses.

A warning notice was served on the occupier of a factory where the chimney smoke had become a nuisance. In 1891 the work was transferred to sanitary authorities and special powers were given to the L.C.C. The Council's coal officers were instructed to report any cases of smoke nuisance that they observed and in the next two years 1381 cases of smoke nuisance were dealt with.

The L.C.C. coal officers also keep a watch on railway engines.

There were 635 prosecutions for smoke nuisance from

Weights and Measures Inspectors

Above: "Whitehall 1-2-1-2"

Below: How London protects its citizens

railway engines between 1889 and 1904 and only thirty-seven between 1932 and 1937, which shows the tremendous advantages brought about by the electrification of the railways.

The L.C.C. asked the Royal Society in 1902 to look into the business of evolving more efficient coal-burning stoves to lessen the nuisance of smoke from dwelling-house chimneys. A Committee was formed and is still devoting its attention to the pollution of the atmosphere by smoke.

In 1926 the L.C.C. made a by-law which provides that the emission of black smoke from factory chimneys for two minutes in any half hour is a nuisance.

As a result of all its work the L.C.C. has certainly made the London air cleaner than it was fifty years ago, but even the L.C.C. is helpless as yet to prevent the sudden descent of a London fog.

In 1891 the staff of the Public Control Department consisted of four clerks and eighty-six inspectors; in 1937, 280 permanent clerks were employed in County Hall and there were about 252 outside inspectors.

Chapter 14　　　　　　　　　LONDON'S SUPPLIES

Few departments of the L.C.C. are more exciting than
that of Supplies, where all the needs of the L.C.C. are
supplied from pins (60,000 oz.) to castor oil (7600 lb.),
sometimes very quickly.

For the evacuation of school children from London in
September 1938 a requisition was made suddenly for 400,000
labels at 11 o'clock in the morning. They were not only
obtained but also distributed ready for attaching to the
bodies of the children by 5 o'clock that same afternoon.

Buying and selling in bulk is always interesting, but the
L.C.C. Supplies Department has to provide everything for
113,000 patients, inmates and staffs of many hospitals
and institutions, and satisfy the educational demands of
800,000 teachers and children.

The L.C.C. first started centralised buying in 1909,
when the Supplies Department was created by amalga-

mating the eight then existing stores which worked independently of each other.

The work was greatly expanded in 1930, when all the work relating to Public Assistance was transferred to the L.C.C.

As well as buying, the Supplies Department is responsible for the condemnation of stores, the disposal of obsolete stocks, the checking of all stocktakings and for various kinds of maintenance work and the rendering of services.

In many ways, you see, it is very like running a vast departmental store. There are two main divisions in the department, (a) administrative and (b) executive.

The administrative work includes the buying of goods, the preparation of estimates of costs, the obtaining of tenders, the checking of accounts of contractors and the preparation of them for payment.

There is a total staff of 1001, and it works in the County Hall and Shell Mex House. There are also many depots.

That at Clerkenwell contains the printing, stationery, books and schools apparatus section; Bloomsbury, the textiles, soft goods, clothing and leather section; Peckham, the food section; Stamford Hill, the furniture, timber and general stores section; and Wandsworth, the repair work of motors. There are three coal depots where coal is received direct from collieries.

Some £4,750,000 was spent in 1937–38 in the acquisition of supplies, of which £1,452,687 was spent on food.

It shows with what scrupulous care goods are treated when we realise that the total value of goods damaged and broken in that year amounted to only £165.

In 1935 the L.C.C. began to buy in bulk certain supplies in connection with the erection of dwellings on the Council's housing estates. It began with enamel baths, portable boilers, mantel register grates, lavatory basins, and internal doors for 2500 houses. Then the scheme was extended to include all buildings, and all sorts of other household fixtures were added.

The milk bill of the year was £242,000. And even window cleaning cost £16,500.

The bill for hair-cutting and shaving, clockwinding and repairing, boiler cleaning, piano and organ tuning, chimney sweeping, vermin destruction, removal of rubbish and things of that sort came to £20,050.

On the other hand, this section of Supplies managed to sell waste materials, hogwash, old metals, rags, clinker and ash for the respectable sum of £28,300, which more than pays the Supplies' laundry bill.

They check all deliveries of meat, poultry and fish at the hospitals and schools as well as the inventories of all the principal departments.

One very large section deals with medical supplies, and here we find them buying 70,000 lb. of liquid paraffin, 26,300 lb. of bicarbonate of soda, and 2,267,000 tablets of aspirin every year.

Supplies Department is responsible for County Hall maintenance, which means keeping 370,000 square feet of glass and 285,000 feet of courtyards, corridors, halls and staircases clean; 100 sacks of waste paper and 110 large dustbins have to be cleared every day.

The buying and distribution of food for 113,000 inmates in 164 institutions is a huge task.

120 tons of goods come into and go out from the Peckham depot every day. The total value of food supplied is about £1,500,000.

Nearly 8,000,000 lb. of meat, 1,500,000 lb. of butter, 1,500,000 lb. of bacon and nearly 10,000,000 eggs, over 4,000,000 lb. of sugar, 2,000,000 lb. of apples, nearly 3,000,000 bananas, 15,500,000 lb. of potatoes, 27,000,000 pints of milk, 3,500,000 lb. of bread, and 3,395,400 cigarettes are bought each year.

Another section of the Supplies Department deals with fuel and fodder and buys 360,000 tons of coal and coke, 350,000 gallons of oil fuel and 2,250,000 bundles of firewood every year.

It also buys 17,200 lb. of sand and seed for birds, over 1,000,000 bulbs and nearly 10,000 packets of flower seeds.

Inmates of the institutions make 36,000 brooms, 15,000 tooth brushes and most of the baskets used by the L.C.C. every year. And saving was also effected by selling 487 tons of waste paper in 1937–38.

Among items of furniture for schools, hospitals and institutions were 7569 beds, 2435 blackboards, 128,940 combs, 1556 tons of soap and nearly 4,000,000 feet of timber.

Over 2000 tons of paper is supplied every year for making up exercise books and printing the 1579 documents and over a million kinds of handbills and pamphlets.

The stationery section, curiously enough, is responsible for the supply of cricket bats, stumps, balls, footballs, wicket-keeping gloves, hockey sticks, stoolball wickets and all other sporting gear as well as books.

2500 cricket bats and nearly 60,000 balls are bought each year. 1,321,650 textbooks and prize books were issued in 1937 and over 6,000,000 exercise books, 5,000,000 paper clips, nearly 20,000,000 envelopes, nearly 2,000,000 pencils, over 5,400,000 pens and 3,800,000 chalks.

In the textile section a brave attempt has been made to get away from standardisation, particularly with regard to women's hats, millinery and needlework material.

By buying seasonal clearing lines a considerable economy has been effected, as the manufacturers naturally prefer to sell to the Council rather than to dispose of them to the trade.

This department supplied nearly 75,000 pairs of boots and shoes, 50,000 aprons, 225,000 tablecloths, 2,000,000 buttons, 2,250,000 needles, 145,000 thimbles, 17,000 pairs of scissors, 700,000 safety pins, 10,000 sets of pyjamas, 44,000 nightgowns, 342,000 yards of cloth, 885,000 yards of calico, 118,000 handkerchiefs and 143,000 pairs of stockings and socks during the year 1937–38.

From this you will see at once, if you have ever tried to buy anything in large quantities, how immense a saving it is to the L.C.C. to keep a special department for this purpose.

BOOKS YOU SHOULD READ

London and its Government. By Sir Percy Harris. (Dent, 3s. 6d.)

London Statistics. Vol. XL, 1935–37. (L.C.C. 15s.)

L.C.C. Report of the Council to 31 *March* 1919. (P. S. King, 5s.)

The London County Council, 1938. (L.C.C. 1s.)

The Silent Social Revolution. By G. A. N. Lowndes. (Oxford University Press, 6s.)

Report of the Metropolitan Board of Works, 1888.

Final Report of the School Board for London, 1870–1904. (P. S. King, 5s.)

History of the L.C.C. By Sir George Gibbon and R. W. Bell. (Macmillan, 21s.)

The Story of the L.C.C. By A. E. Davies. (Williams and Norgate, 2s. 6d.)

How Greater London is Governed. By H. S. Morrison. (Peter Davies, 6s.)

BUCKINGHAM

HERTF

Potters Bar

Rickma nsworth

Barnet

Harrow

Hendon

Wembley

ES

Denham

Uxbridge

Ealing

LO

BERKS.

Kew

Staines

Richmond

Wimbledon Common

Thames

Hampton

Chertsey

Bushey Park

Esher

Nonesuch Park

Crawley
10

SURREY

Ockham Common

Epsom

15

Dorking

Reigate

Guildford

20

The Growth of
LONDON
Built-up Area 1889: black
Built-up Area 1939: —
County of London: green

For EU product safety concerns, contact us at Calle de José Abascal, 56–1°,
28003 Madrid, Spain or eugpsr@cambridge.org.

www.ingramcontent.com/pod-product-compliance
Ingram Content Group UK Ltd.
Pitfield, Milton Keynes, MK11 3LW, UK
UKHW020308140625
459647UK00014B/1793